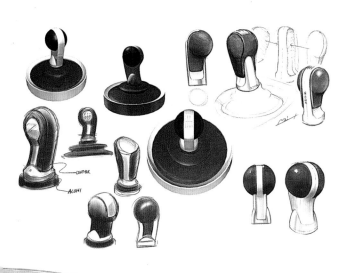

GW00645215

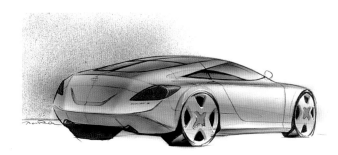

Nissan 350Z

Behind the Resurrection of a Legend

John Lamm

MOTORBOOKS
INTERNATIONAL

This edition first published in 2003 by Motorbooks International, an imprint of MBI Publishing Company, Galtier Plaza, Suite 200, 380 Jackson Street, St. Paul, MN 55101-3885 USA

The information in this book is true and complete to the best of our knowledge. All recommendations are made without any guarantee on the part of the author or Publisher, who also disclaim any liability incurred in connection with the use of this data or specific details.

We recognize that some words, model names and designations, for example, mentioned herein are the property of the trademark holder. We use them for identification purposes only. This is not an official publication.

Motorbooks International titles are also available at discounts in bulk quantity for industrial or sales-promotional use. For details write to Special Sales Manager at Motorbooks International Wholesalers & Distributors, Galtier Plaza, Suite 200, 380 Jackson Street, St. Paul, MN 55101-3885 USA.

ISBN 0-7603-1575-2

On the front cover: The 350Z in bronze. *John Lamm*

On the endpapers: A variety of early concept drawings. *Nissan*

On the frontispiece: An early sketch for the 350Z touching on its 240Z roots. *Nissan*

On the title page: The 2003 350Z in dark silver. *John Lamm*

On the back cover: The 350Z in dark blue. *John Lamm* A cutaway drawing and engine illustration show the underpinnings of the car. *Nissan*

Editor: Lee Klancher
Designer: LeAnn Kuhlmann

Printed in China

Contents

Introduction

The Z car and I go way back. We both started in the business at about the same time, untested neophytes. I went through my first race-driving school in a Z car when Bob Bondurant still used them at Sears Point Raceway, and I watched as Paul Newman used a Z to win his SCCA championship in 1978.

I photographed the first, then-secret, 300ZX in 1984, before it was shown to the world. I was with the initial wave of journalists stunned by the beauty of the last-generation 300ZX . . . and was as upset as any automotive journalist when the car was killed.

That was it—there's no hope for Nissan now, we thought. Have they forgotten what the Z meant to all of us—and apparently to many of them? Go ahead, we thought, rip your heart out if you must. . . .

But after a period when we almost wrote Nissan off, we began to hear rumors. The Z might be back . . . maybe . . . well, it could happen . . . and then it did.

Thank heavens.

What's as fascinating about the revival of the Z car itself is what the rebirth says about the automobile industry.

On the one hand, it's a business of numbers. Numbers that represent the dimensions of the cars it builds . . . precise measurements that allow the thousands of pieces in any car to fit together.

Numbers that reflect the sales of those cars in monthly and annual reports. Numbers that represent value, both in the cost of the cars to buyers and in the company's stock price. Numbers that show profit.

Numbers, numbers, numbers—and yet they are only one gauge of success in the automotive industry. That's because buying a car so often has a little to do with numbers and a lot to do with emotion.

Few buyers fall in love with payment books, but many fall for the curve of a fender, the rumble of an exhaust, a flash of red in the periphery of their vision, or, perhaps, the memory of a promise they made to themselves a long time ago.

So, while it probably made sense to kill the Z car in the mid-1990s as sport utility vehicles rose from the mire, it was also a mistake.

When you talk with those who worked at Nissan and Nissan Design International during those tough years, you come to appreciate how depressing smothering the Z to death was and what a tonic its rebirth is to an entire corporation as the lead car in a full-scale product revival.

As a parallel, look at the effect on General Motors of hiring Bob Lutz as their product guru, a man unafraid to talk openly, to deride doing business as it was, and to set fire to ghosts in the corporate closet.

Luckily for Nissan, it has its own guru, in the form of Carlos Ghosn . . . a rare man indeed, the sort who can take a corporation of tens of thousands and, in short order, reset its compass. Make no mistake, the groundwork for the Z car was already in place when Ghosn arrived on the scene, but he laid out the challenge to make it as good as it is, to prod the engineers, stroke the designers, inspire the marketers, give the dealers and Nissan employees the hope they needed.

The result is one of the most exciting sports cars on the market today: the Nissan 350Z.

Read on.

—John Lamm

The 350Z is more than just a car for Nissan—it is the result of a company pulling itself out of tough times to come up with a winner.

1

From 240Z to 300ZX

Fond Memories, Difficult Times

These days, Japanese cars are highly respected for their efficient, intelligent designs, excellent workmanship, and legendary reliability; but in 1970, Americans didn't fully trust them.

Although some Japanese products had established themselves as well-designed, high-quality brands—Nikon cameras being an excellent example—we were still wary of vehicles with names like Bluebird and Patrol. But an ever-growing chorus claimed these cars from Japan were getting to be quite good—well made and reliable. Still, buying small, not-too-expensive, Japanese-made manufactured goods was one thing, but what about a commodity as big and pricey as an automobile?

Then there were unpatriotic aspects of buying a car from Japan, though this didn't seem to be a problem with cars from Germany or Italy.

Into this socioeconomic scenario came Mr. K.

His full name is Yutaka Katayama, and he's the man who established Datsun—now Nissan—in the United States. Although the first Datsuns were shipped to the states in 1958, by the mid-1960s they still hadn't reached great numbers. That's when Mr. K arrived. He had developed a thorough understanding of the United States and its auto-buying public. By means of advertising, word of mouth, and continually improving products, he was able to

gradually but firmly establish in the minds of consumers, the company's light trucks and sedans as vehicles to own.

It says a great deal about Mr. K's efforts and influence that in 1998 he was inducted into the U.S. Automotive Hall of Fame in Dearborn, Michigan; a few decades before that, you could have been publicly put down in that city just for buying a Japanese car.

As of 1967, Mr. K was able to throw a little fun into the Datsun sales equation with a sports car. Called the 2000 Roadster, it was not unlike another popular sports car of the time, the MGB. With its 150 bhp engine and a 5-speed manual transmission, the 2000 was a good-performing, reasonably priced machine.

From the start, Datsun put the Roadster on the race track, which was crucial to selling in that sports-car market segment back then. The year it debuted, the 2000 won the first of its 10 national championships in the Sports Car Club of America.

Only the Beginning

The year before the 2000 Roadster was introduced to the U.S., Datsun designers and engineers in Japan were already working on its replacement. This time, Nissan wouldn't go after the MG market but would essentially take on the image and feel of the Jaguar XK-E, with a

One of the historic design elements on the futuristic-looking 350Z is the front grille with its wide rectangular opening like those of the early Z cars.

The layout design of the Z was dictated as much by history as it was practicality. The designers made the car a hatchback, just like the original Z cars, even though the hatch was an engineering challenge.

Below: Datsun's 240Z had a marked impact on the sports car market, offering style and speed (0–60 in 8.7 seconds) for $3,526 at a time when Alfa Romeo's GT and Volvo's P1800 were about $4,500.

price 40 percent below that of the famed British sports car.

Heresy in the minds of many, but just the ticket for Mr. K, who was said to be an E-Type fan.

By October 1969, the new sports car was ready, tagged with the name 240Z. Why that name? Because it was popular at the time to have a number in the name of a sports car, usually one that referred to the car's engine displacement, and Zs had a 2.4-liter six. According to Mr. K, "Z can be taken to mean so many things—zenith, for example—and sounds good in almost any language." In Japan, the sports car was (and is) named the Fairlady Z.

From the start, the Z was a sensation. Then as now, *Road & Track* was considered the authoritative voice when it comes to sports cars. It was so excited by the Z that it ran a black-and-white cover in January 1970, just to get the new Datsun on the cover in a timely fashion.

The new Z's appeal began with its exterior, which originated as a shape from famed European designer Albrecht Goertz (Goertz also designed the 1957 BMW 507, the visual grandfather of BMW's modern Z8). With its long hood and short deck with a hatchback, the steel unit-body shape finalized by Nissan's studios was detailed just right. About the only disappointing aspect was the hubcaps, but luckily, with all the Z parts inherited from other Datsuns, aftermarket wheels made for the 2000 Roadster by companies like Minilite and American Racing bolted right on.

Inside, the 240Z was considered on a par with its contemporaries, with good white-in-back instrumentation, supportive seats, and equipment not normally standard in those days, such as an AM radio with electric antenna, carpeting, a rear window defroster, and even a real wood steering wheel.

Japanese automakers had (and some still have) an almost mind-numbing array of different models, so Nissan was able to draw from a deep parts bin for the 240Z, which was critical to keeping the price down. While the new sports car had a unique independent rear suspension, the front design was lifted from the 1800 sedan and the brakes from the 2000 Roadster, all appropriately reworked for the Z car's size and purpose.

Under the long Z hood was a 2.4-liter, single-overhead-camshaft straight-6 that was essentially the 4-cylinder powerplant in the (now legendary) 510 sedan,

The engine displacement of the 280Z was up to 2.8 liters, and the straight-6 offered fuel injection to help meet new 1975 emissions regulations, which were sapping performance from automobiles.

*Winding along the
California coast,
the 350Z meeting
your greatest power
and handling needs—
inviting, isn't it?*

Styling of the Z car changed for the 1979 model year with the 280ZX (black) and again in the early 1980s with the debut of the 300ZX, the first major alteration of the Z formula.

Not only was the 300ZX an excellent-handling car, but it had outstanding raw acceleration, with the twin-turbo, manual-gearbox option taking the car to 60 mph in just 6.2 tire-smoking seconds.

with two extra cylinders. The 150 bhp at 6,000 rpm and 148 ft-lb of torque were routed through a 4-speed manual transmission (a 5-speed was optional, as was a late-intro 3-speed automatic).

Those of us who were at the Nissan press conference during the 2002 Detroit Auto Show and heard the stunned

murmuring that followed the announcement of the 350Z's very favorable pricing structure quickly recalled that a temptingly low price has been as much a part of the car's heritage as the hatchback and Z name.

With a 1970 base price of $3,526, the independent-rear-suspension 240Z was a bargain compared to such contemporary live-rear-axle Grand Touring (GT) sports car stalwarts as Alfa Romeo's 132-bhp GTV at $4,500, MGB's 92-bhp GT at $3,000, Opel's 102-bhp GT at $3,500, and Volvo's 130-bhp P1800E at $4,500. The Datsun even stood up reasonably well against the likes of a $7,000 Mercedes-Benz 280SL and Porsche's $6,000 911T.

Put through *Road & Track*'s performance trials for the April 1970 issue, the Datsun proved it was more than just a nice marketing package, getting to 60 mph in 8.7 seconds, beating the Alfa GTV by 1.2 seconds and the Opel GT by 2.1 seconds, and just outdoing the then-new Porsche 914/4 on the skidpad by generating 0.72 g. Top speed in this 4-speed model was 122 mph, and fuel mileage was 21.0 mpg.

Just as important for Datsun, perhaps, were the first and last words in the *R&T* road test. The first, the subhead, read, "New standards in performance and elegance for medium-priced 2-seat GT cars." The last were two prophetic sentences that squarely addressed then current thinking about Japanese cars: "The Japanese industry is no longer borrowing anything from other nations. In fact, a great struggle may be ahead just to prevent a complete reversal of that cliché."

Over the next years, the Z car developed a solid following, despite potential buyers often waiting months on a dealer's list to get one. A *Road & Track* owner's survey two years into the Z car's life had 91 percent willing to buy another.

But legislation was hurting the Datsun the same way it was emasculating all the performance cars of the era. Safety rules called for better occupant protection. Hardware, such as larger bumpers, added weight—130 pounds in the Z's case. Worse yet, automakers were just beginning to struggle with serious regs meant to lower engine emissions. By 1973, the 240Z's horsepower was down to 129 and torque to 127 ft-lb. A Z tested late that year needed 11.9 seconds to get to 60 mph.

Enter the 260Z

Visually unaltered from the 240, the 260Z was offered for 1974. The additional 200 cc of engine displacement (with other engine changes) brought horsepower to 139, torque to 137 ft-lb, and the 0 to 60 time back down to

10.0 seconds. Although the price had climbed to $4,995, *R&T* was still able to write, "At $5,000 the 260Z is almost as impressive a value in terms of 1974 dollars as the 240Z was at $3,500 in 1970."

That same year brought a new body style, the 2+2. From the nose back to the front end of the door, the Z was the same, but aft of there, designers added "occasional" small seats for two people, most likely children. Wheelbase went from 90.7 inches to 102.6,

With the ZX—now a Nissan, not a Datsun— the sports car took a turn toward luxury, its interior still sporty but softened a bit.

Another big change with the ZX was the move from a straight-6 to a naturally aspirated 3.0-liter V-6 with 160 horsepower or, as shown here, a 200-horsepower with turbocharger, which knocked the 0–60 mph time down to the mid-7-seconds range.

Nissan altered the Z-car formula still more with the 1990 model year's 300ZX. Handling was vastly improved, with the hard-edged character of the old ZX replaced with smoother, more highly refined suspensions.

A new 300ZX was powered by one of two engines: a 3.0-liter, 24-valve V-6 with 222 horsepower or a twin-turbo version that offered a blistering 300 horsepower when matched with a 5-speed manual transmission.

overall length to 180.9, curb weight to 2,855 pounds, and the price to $5,750.

Performance suffered, of course, but this newest Z car opened up a market for families with small children. This began a tradition that lasted right through the 300ZX in 1996, though abandoned with the 350Z, with that segment essentially taken by the Infiniti G35 Sport Coupe.

The 260Z was a short-lived interim model. Datsun came back for 1975 with the 280Z, not only raising engine displacement from 2565 cc to 2754 to earn its new name number, but swapping the straight-6's pair of Hitachi-SU carburetors for a Japanese-made-and-licensed version of Bosch's L-Jetronic fuel injection. Weight also went up, but with horsepower back at 149 and torque up to 163 ft-lb, performance was almost back to 240Z numbers. Despite ever-tightening emissions rules, 60 mph clocked in at 9.4 seconds. Price was also up again, to $6,284, climbing continually higher in that time of inflation and dollar/yen parity problems.

With all the noisy nitpicking now between the government, public-interest groups, and the auto industry over relatively small proposed changes in emissions and fuel economy standards, it's easy to forget the profound changes in the 1970s and 1980s to lower emissions and increases in the safety of occupants. Regulations and fuel crises in the mid- and late-1970s also put enormous emphasis on fuel economy as gasoline prices shot up dramatically.

Many automakers seemed to be running for their corporate lives just to keep up. Sports cars from large automakers, such as the Z and Chevrolet's Corvette, went through little visual change as engineers scrambled to integrate rapidly changing safety and emissions rules. Yet for the 1979 model year, Datsun debuted a new Z, the 280ZX, which altered the sports car's formula.

The 280ZX

Dimensional changes in the 2-seater were minimal—less than an extra inch of length and height—and curb weight was down by a bit, but the character of the Z changed. Where the original Zs were sporty and lusty, the new 280ZX was rather more luxurious and genteel, arguably yielding up the Japanese seat-of-the-pants sports car segment to Mazda's impressive new RX-7.

Exterior styling was not all that different, just crisper and looking even wider than the additional 1.5 inches would suggest. Inside, the changes were more dramatic. The basics, such as the three central gauges, remained, but the general look and feel was of a more expensive automobile. The seats received a serious upgrading, though those in the back of the 2+2 were still for children.

Nissan designed both 2-seat and 2+2 layouts for the 300ZX, and it was one of those rare occasions when the longer-wheelbase version of a sports car looked as good as the two-seater.

DATSUN 280·ZZZAP

Nissan again went to its parts bin for the underpinnings of the ZX, which were adapted from the 810 big sedan. The driveline was a carryover, with a 135 bhp inline-6 and a 5-speed manual or 3-speed automatic transmission, the former getting to 60 mph in 9.2 seconds.

Prices had taken another jump—the 2-seater was just under $10,000, with a well-equipped 2+2 around $12,000—but *Road & Track* commented, "In its new upmarket price class, the ZX does offer impressive value for the dollar. . . ."

The ZX brought Z performance back in line with the original 240, but Datsun kicked its sports car up into the Corvette category in 1980. One of the favored new tools to boost performance as engineers learned more about meeting emissions rules was the turbocharger. Datsun jumped right in with the 280ZX Turbo.

Thanks to the exhaust-driven supercharger, horsepower jumped to 180 and, perhaps more significant, torque went to 203 ft-lb at 2800 rpm. Though only a 3-speed automatic transmission was offered, the combination was enough to squirt the ZX Turbo to 60 mph in just 7.4 seconds, almost 2 seconds quicker than Porsche's 924 Turbo and nearly a half second quicker than the Corvette.

Heady stuff for the Z car, which went through significant chassis changes to make it more in tune with recently acquired power. This was new territory for Nissan's highly regarded sports car . . . not only was it quicker than a 'Vette, but at about $16,500, it was also more expensive than Chevrolet's famous fiberglass car.

Other changes were in store as the Z car passed into its second decade—more luxury, a removable T-top roof, and still more accessories—but it was increasingly apparent that Nissan needed to do a more complete reworking of the successful Z-car formula.

Besides, although the Z would hit a total sales figure approaching three-quarters of a million units, sales had begun to slip in the early 1980s with competition such as the Toyota Supra and Mazda RX-7.

The 300ZX and Datsun's Name Change

Enter the 300ZX and a name switch, the company dropping the Datsun label and taking the one used in the rest of the world: Nissan.

There was no mistaking that this new model was a Z car, even though it had been through a complete restyling, including flip-up headlights. Size and weight were in the same ballpark as the 280ZX, and the suspensions were still independent at both ends, using MacPherson struts fore and semi-trailing arms at the back. Again there were 2-place and 2+2 body styles.

What separated the 300ZX from the older models as much as the styling was in the engine compartment. The traditional inline-6 was gone, replaced by a new 3.0-liter, single-overhead-cam V-6, available with either 160 bhp and 174 ft-lb of torque or, optionally, a turbo version, with a solid 200 bhp and 227 ft-lb of torque. The important 0 to 60 mph times were under 9.0 seconds for the normally aspirated engine, and the turbo 300ZX was easily in the mid-7-second range.

Nissan's sports car was now regularly compared to the Corvette and Porsches, and its prices reflected the move uptown, starting at $20,000 and reaching $26,000 on a well-done turbo.

From the very first 240Z through this first-generation 300ZX, the continuing family ties among the Z cars were easy to see. It was all quite evolutionary, and with good reason. The package sold strongly, starting with 15,988 240Zs in 1970. From 1974 through 1986 (except for 1975,

a generally tough year), Datsun, then Nissan, sold more than 55,000 Z cars annually, peaking with an exceptional 86,007 in 1979. Toward the end of the 1980s, however, the Z formula had begun to thin, so Nissan designed and developed a totally new 300ZX for the 1990 model year.

Arguably, it was the best of all the early Zs. The exterior design was sensational, a thing of beauty in either 2-seat or 2+2 configuration. From the 1993 model year, you could buy the first official, factory-certified Z-car convertible, though they were not as beautiful as the coupes.

Inside, the car was like a sports luxury car compared to its predecessors, yet the chassis was as finely crafted as the 300ZX's exterior. All the latest modern thinking was there, from suspension geometry to super-HICAS (High Capacity Actively Controlled Steering), which was essentially 4-wheel steering.

Nissan hired the highly regarded American race driver/engineer Ron Grable to assist in developing and

The 350Z came about after an exhaustive series of design concepts that gave the new Z distinctive lines and a unique, modern look.

Nissan Zs were very successful racing in the IMSA series, winning seven manufacturer's titles and driven by eight series-championship drivers. This is a 1993 300ZX IMSA car being raced by Steve Millen. Nissan

tuning the suspension, with excellent results. Those of us on the original press launch of the 300ZX in Japan will never forget the back-to-back drive against the now-outmoded first-generation 300ZX, which felt hard-edged and downright antique compared to the new 300ZX.

Its performance was more than just handling. Nissan offered a pair of engine choices, a normally aspirated 24-valve 3.0-liter V-6 with 222 bhp or everyone's dream machine, the twin-turbo edition, with 300 bhp if you had the 5-speed manual or 280 bhp matched to the 4-speed automatic. Z-car acceleration numbers dove again, down to around 8.0 seconds with the normal V-6 and a tire-smoking 6.2 with the turbo engine. A wonderful automobile, it was an almost annual resident of *Car and Driver*'s 10 Best list, and arguably one of the best used-sports-car bargains today.

Just one little problem. In its day, the 300ZX didn't sell all that well. It was pricey, a situation made difficult by the ever-changing dollar-yen relationship, with the car's original cost running in the $40,000-and-up category.

After selling at the low 20,000-per-year level for its first seasons, sales of the 300ZX began a long downward slide, to just 1,142 in 1997 and 289 in its final year, 1998. Ironically, one of the last of these models was installed in Los Angeles' Petersen Automotive Museum.

No one wanted to see the Z car disappear, and many at Nissan considered it the company's philosophical heart. But Nissan had bigger problems than the sinking Z. Selling automobiles can be a cyclical business, and when the cycle heads down because a company's products are out of phase and irrelevant, it's a slippery slope indeed.

Nissan's Problems

Those failing sales of the Z were symbolic of what was happening with the rest of Nissan's models. Around the automotive world, Nissan's very future was in question.

It seemed impossible that one of the great Japanese automakers, the first to tap the U.S. market, was in a near-fatal dive, yet here it was. Who could save Nissan?

How about the French?

It seemed an odd pairing at first glance, but with further inspection, a tie-up between Nissan and France's Renault made sense. For one thing, their market strengths were complementary. Where Renault was popular in Western and Eastern Europe, the Middle East, the Mediterranean, North Africa, and the Latin American countries, Nissan had a strong presence in Japan, North America, Southeast Asia, and Central America.

Their product lineups were reasonably complementary, and they would have significant production facilities around the world. Combined, the two companies would instantly become the fourth largest automaker in the world, producing 4.8 million vehicles to take 9.1 percent of the globe's auto market.

That's what happened on March 27, 1999. The two automakers signed an agreement that had Renault paid $6.5 billion for a 36.8 percent stake in Nissan, Japan (upped to 44.4 percent in March 2002), 22.5 percent of Nissan Diesel, and all of Nissan's financial subsidiaries in Europe.

More important, perhaps, Renault quickly appointed Carlos Ghosn, a 44-year-old Brazilian, as chief operating officer of Nissan. A year later he added the title of president, having already proved that any concerns about cultural clashes were unfounded. Where attempts to redirect the efforts of a huge automaker are equated to trying to dock the *Queen Mary* with a rowboat, Ghosn essentially picked up the *Queen Mary*, spun her around in midair, and set her back down.

Most relevant to this story, however, is that Carlos Ghosn was also a former 300ZX driver. . . .

Z cars were raced in the United States from their first days. Over the years, many Z cars were raced by privateers. Also, the factory originally backed Bob Sharp on the East Coast and Peter Brock—and then Don Devendorf's Electromotive—on the West Coast. Best known of all the Z drivers was actor Paul Newman, who is seen here winning his 1979 C Production Championship at the SCCA runoffs at Road Atlanta.

2

Preaching Revival in a Time of Fear

How Would You Save a Failing Corporation?

On July 1, 2000, the day of his sixtieth birthday, Jerry Hirshberg packed it in. After 20 years guiding Nissan Design International (NDI, now called NDA, for Nissan Design America), the automaker's renowned studio near the posh San Diego suburb of La Jolla, Hirshberg turned over the studio keys to Tom Semple. Though Hirshberg retained a consultancy with the corporation, he went off to enjoy his passions for art and the clarinet.

He departed a happy guy, for while Nissan was still struggling to regain its reputation and market share, Hirshberg had a strong sense the company had turned a corner—that it would survive nicely in its new relationship with Renault. Besides, he knew the Z car would be back: "I see that car as my swan song. It's just a happy note to have gone out on, and made my retirement a lot sweeter."

There was nothing happy or sweet, however, about life at Nissan just a few years earlier, when the famous 300ZX was pulled from the automaker's lineup.

"I can't speak for the entire corporation, but I can speak for my perceptions," Hirshberg recalls. "NDI was just crushed by that information. Other cars that were kind of our signature, sporty cars of all kinds, had gone away, and the Z car was the last vestige of a corporation that used to

believe in itself and was in touch with why in the hell it was in this business to begin with.

"To our way of thinking, we had killed off a part of our soul, a part that defined what we were . . . so it seemed that with the worsening times economically, this was just a bad idea, even though it could be justified economically."

Killing the Z made sense on the balance sheets. As Hirshberg points out, "We were not alone in recognizing that at that time sports cars were just as dead as they could be . . . we were selling Zs down in the hundreds rather than thousands. On the other hand, we never thought the function of a sports car was to carry the organization on its back economically. It was to beat a path, to shine a halo around us and be the sparkplug for the whole line. Without it, we were a faceless corporation operating under what some folks in marketing called the three-sedan plan. Just a maker of sedans. It was pretty depressing.

"There was actually concern floating around that we might not be in business much longer and a deeper belief that at the very least we would not be alone for very long, that someone else would have to take over. The French had not yet come into the picture, though there were

Viewing a 350Z from behind emphasizes the muscular haunches of its shape and conjures thoughts of a powerful sports car.

These are just a few of the many sketches that represent the early thinking about the forthcoming Z car. While virtually every designer at Nissan Design International contributed, these are mainly from Jerry Hirshberg, who retired from the firm in July 2000, and his successor, Tom Semple. Hirshberg's ideas show a decided retro feeling, while Semple's pushed the Z car in a more modern direction. Nissan

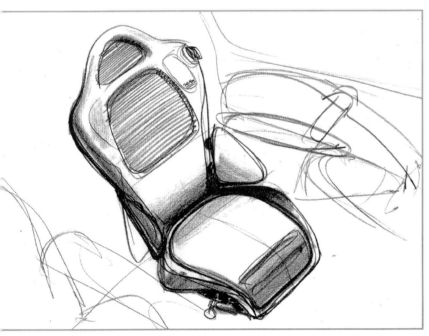

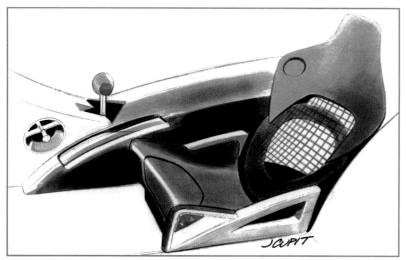

rumors all over the place over whether it would be Renault or, at that time, Daimler-Benz."

What to do? Hirshberg held a meeting at NDI and gathered all the designers and key managers. The purpose of the meeting was to ask a single question to which he did not have an answer. "The question was, 'If any of you were running the corporation, what would you do now to turn things around?' Then we went around the room and gave everybody a chance to speak out. There were about 20 people there, and everybody gave responsible, cogent answers as to what they would do if they were running the organization. When it got around to me, I said, 'I'd bring back the Z.' "

Those at the meeting asked Hirshberg to explain why. He replied, "Because by just involving ourselves in such a labor of love, it would literally, without any preaching, remind us of what the right priorities are in this business. That it is, in truth, an irrational business . . . or at least nonrational, in the sense that most of the time nobody *really* needs a new car. We buy them for emotional reasons, and we [Nissan] have gotten out of the emotion business." He added, "It would not only remind the public of who we are, it would by our sheer involvement remind *us* of who we are."

Hirshberg went on to point out that making a sports car was something Nissan was terrifically good at,

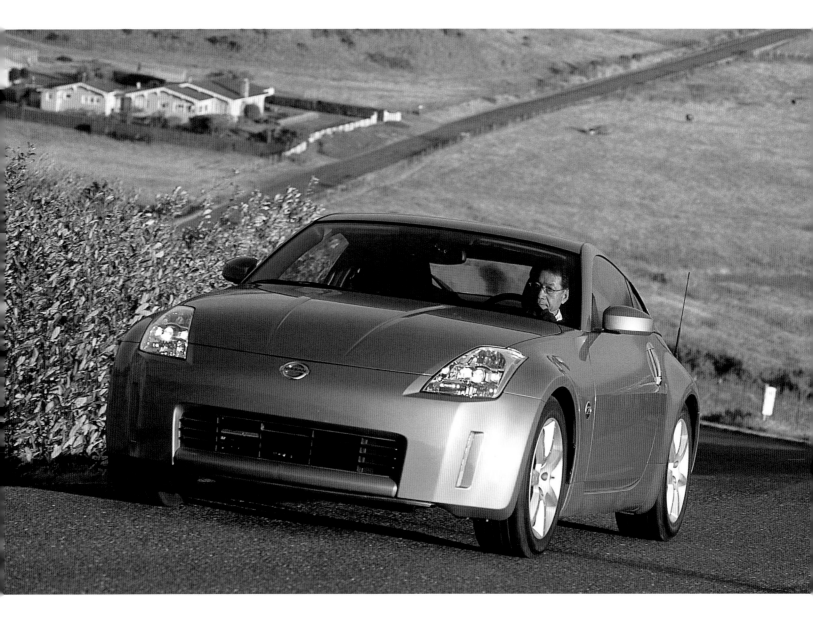

especially among the Japanese companies. "From my point of view, having two legendary Zs in your history is something that organizations such as Honda or Toyota would kill for. And here we were, just letting it lie. So we had currency in the bank, and this was the time to spend it.

"The argument at the time, of course,. . . and what I first heard from Nissan when we started talking about reviving the Z . . . was a reminder that this was a time to concentrate on bread and butter, not toys. But it seemed to me that this toy was essential food for this badly weakened organization."

So without an official number, project name, or support, NDI began a program to redesign the Z car. Hirshberg points out that the strongest voice design had at

that point within the corporation was not verbal but visual. So they self-assigned the project and said, "Let's just see what a new Z would look like."

But studio time is expensive, and the project had no budget. Who would pay?

"When we were assigned to other projects," Hirshberg goes on, "we just double-assigned ourselves. We simply added between the cracks . . . rather than a coffee break or a full lunch hour, we started sketching and doing scale-model Zs with clay.

"Before a car is a prototype, it's just a question of creative time. And so I suppose you could say we were living on the funds that were coming from other projects, but I had crafted an arrangement when I was originally

Dramatic, advanced styling became a major goal for the 350Z, the aim being to establish a new style that would not only attract new-car buyers, but also set a theme for all vehicles from the automaker.

involved in founding NDI that we would be free to do other projects, such as nonautomotive products and cars that we felt strongly about, that we could then present to Nissan." So the project was done aboveboard, but "we didn't feel it was the right time to talk about it. We just went ahead and did it."

The designers decided to explore their own directions and then choose the strongest design. They didn't really know what they would do with it, except that they would begin to show it and go full-size. When you go full-size with something, it's no longer hidden.

"I wasn't really doing it secretly, I just wasn't asking for approval at that point. I felt the corporation was in disarray."

The Road Show

Good luck played a part in the next step. At the time, Nissan's head of public relations was Jason Vines, a well-respected PR man who could probably make a nice living

These photos show an under-construction, freshly painted, and ready-to-be-finished-and-detailed Z Concept being prepped for the 1999 Detroit Auto Show. **Nissan**

TAKING THE SHOW
ON THE ROAD

Jason Vines has an indomitable spirit, so when you ask him about the atmosphere at Nissan during the tough days when he was just getting started as the head of public relations, he doesn't come back with the expected answer. He says this: "Dismal yet exciting, because we knew what we had to do, and when the patient's chest is open and you have your hands on the heart, it can be kind of fun."

Soon after Vines started at Nissan on April 1, 1998, one of his veteran staff members, Tim Gallagher, suggested that Vines visit NDI to meet the man in charge there, Jerry Hirshberg. The PR and design chiefs hit it off right away, Hirshberg introducing him to the NDI design staff and showing him some of the projects they had going on at the time.

Among the proposals was a scale model of an SUT (Sport Utility Truck), though there were no plans to build it. Vines looked at the designer and said, "Okay, where's the Z?"

Hirshberg put his finger to his head and said, "It's right here."

"Well, can you take it out?"

Hirshberg said he could, but they had neither budget nor approval to do so. Vines, however, had an idea. He returned to Nissan, met with Mike Seergy, the head of the Nissan division, and made a suggestion.

Vines is a graduate of the very successful Chrysler public relations system, working there back when the automaker was in deep trouble, much as Nissan was in the late 1990s. He revived an idea from that time, when Chrysler was struggling but believed in what it had coming in the near future: create a road show. This traveling exhibit would mean taking executives and future product on the road to show influential people what the company had coming near term, hoping to raise their confidence in Nissan. He likes to paraphrase Lee Iacocca: "Take a peek under the kimono and see what we've got coming. There's a future here."

Seergy bought into the idea of getting out and energizing the media and the analysts, but, more important, Nissan's dealers and employees. To inform them, Vines explains that "we understand what Nissan is all about. It's passion, it's fun . . . it's the Japanese car company with an attitude." The plan was to display the Z car and SUT clay models plus the upcoming Xterra, Maxima, and Sentra production vehicles to these employees, dealers, and opinion leaders.

They got internal resistance, but Seergy stuck with the idea and wanted to know what sort of budget the road show would require. Vines checked with Metalcrafters, the Fountain Valley, California, firm that's world famous for its high-quality prototypes, to determine the cost of the pair of clays. The bill would be some one million dollars. Seergy said he could find only about $900,000, but they moved ahead with the project.

By now it was mid-May, 1998. Vines went back to Hirshberg and said they needed to get the two design ideas into full-size clays quickly. Metalcrafters managed to do the clays in just three weeks, though a money crunch intervened. There was no way they could do complete Z and SUT clays for the allotted money in that short timeframe. The answer? They just finished three sides of the vehicles and left the fourth in rough clay. Vines used this as an excuse to call them "works in progress."

The road show opened in New York City, mainly to financial analysts and dealers, and Vines recalls that a few of the latter had tears in their eyes. He also points out that possibly more important than the Z's actual design was the fact that it was there, that people were able to say, "They get it—this is about the resurgence of Nissan."

From there, the show moved to Smyrna, Tennessee, the site of Nissan's huge manufacturing facility, then to Detroit and Los Angeles.

The road show proved very successful and created a lot of buzz, not only within the company but also in both the financial and journalistic communities. This demonstration in the summer of 1998 also proved to be the start of the buildup for the Detroit Show in January 1999, which was to be Nissan's coming-out party and the day they officially showed the Z car proposal.

Money Appeared

In the aftermath of the road show, there was so much enthusiasm that money appeared—some of it from Japan—to transform the clays into running prototypes for Detroit. Everyone was pumped, dying to work on the new Z and anxiously awaiting its unveiling at the Detroit Show in January.

Just one problem. That show will always be remembered as the "year of the big snow." The weekend before the show opened, a record-setting blizzard swept through the Midwest and paralyzed the region, including Detroit. Air travelers had their flights canceled or dramatically delayed. Executives and journalists by the score couldn't get to Motown and watched show coverage from hotel rooms in New York, Atlanta, Las Vegas, or wherever their airlines and the weather stranded them.

Jason Vines says, "I was suppose to leave on Saturday and was sitting in my home in Newport Beach on Friday night. I called Northwest and was told my flight had been canceled and I couldn't get to Detroit until Tuesday at the earliest. I started crying. This was what we had worked for. We'd invested a lot of time, money, sweat, and fighting to get to this point." As he also observes, "Some people were trying to derail us along the way." Yet after all that, he was stuck in California, despondent, unable to get to weather-beaten Detroit.

Nissan's travel agent offered to look into renting a plane and was back in minutes, saying he could get them a private jet out of Los Angeles.

"Oh God," Vines groaned. "How much?"

"Forty thousand dollars."

Not the sort of news you want to hear when you work for a company in serious financial straits. Vines winced but said he'd call back in five minutes and called his boss, Minoru Nakamura, at home. Nakamura headed Nissan North America and is a man for whom Vines has great respect.

Nakamura answered and said, "We are having trouble getting to Detroit."

"I've got a way," Vines told him. "We can get a private jet."

"How much?"

"Forty thousand dollars."

Nakamura paused, then asked, "Have you got room for me?"

It was a four-hour flight to Detroit, followed by another four-hour journey through the snowbound airport and city to their hotel . . . but they were there.

And they were one of the stars of the Detroit Show, this money-strapped company that some predicted was headed for the door. They ruled the roost, scoring pages of favorable press reports, thanks to the Z and SUT.

The next step was the New York Auto Show in early April 1999, the plan being that after showing the drivable prototype in Detroit, they would announce the Z's production in New York.

The night before the Big Apple presentation, Nakamura called Vines to tell him that top management at Nissan wasn't ready to announce Z production plans, feeling that they had been backed into a corner. Vines told his boss, "If we don't get approval to do this, I'm going to go on a hunger strike!"

Nakamura came back with, "Jason, no one cares if you go on a hunger strike." But he added, "Don't worry, I'll work it out." At three in the morning he called Vines to confirm that, yes, they could announce that the Z would live.

Taking a theme from *Field of Dreams* and, quite literally, a page from *Road & Track*, the New York press show was staged in a fake cornfield. *R&T* features editor Sam Mitani, writing of the Z, quoted the famous line from the movie: "If you build it, they will come." And there was Nakamura, sitting on a bench by the faux corn, reading from a huge copy of *R&T*.

He put down the magazine and announced in a loud voice, "We will build it!" At which point the cornfield opened, and there was the car. The Z would live again . . . and the crowd loved it.

In the end, the move cost Nakamura, who was sent back to a job in Japan. Later, Vines had dinner with his former boss and apologized for painting him into a corner with the Z proposal.

Nakamura smiled and replied, "Jason, don't give yourself so much credit. I allowed myself to be painted into the corner. I had to approve all that stuff . . . we knew what we were doing."

Vines says of Nakamura, "He's a great man. Ghosn saved Nissan in the end, and Nakamura had a hand doing so in North America . . . without question. A brave man."

And a major reason the 350Z exists.

as a standup comedian and, Hirshberg explains, "not a guy who necessarily automatically marched to the corporate drum. There was a natural rapport between us, and we felt similarly about Nissan in the sense that, yes we were in major trouble, but we had the assets and the power to turn this thing around."

Vines' concern was the company's image with the press, financial analysts, the public, and those who worked with the firm. For example, when he dealt with Nissan's salespeople, it became obvious they were losing dealers right and left. Dealers who stayed lacked confidence, disenchanted with the direction Nissan was headed.

Hirshberg recounts, "Jason had called to say they were putting together what he called a road show. They were going to take some concept cars—two or three, hopefully—around the country to four to five key cities, where they were going to gather everybody together and, rather than just have a pep talk, say, 'Here are some things we're thinking about.'

"He wanted to know if we had any concept cars, and I said, 'Funny you should call. . . .' " They got together for lunch and brainstormed. If Vines could find the funding,

Hirshberg could produce the design . . . just what they needed for the road show.

When you look at photos of those first Z proposals—the initial clay and the 1999 Detroit Show car—don't start searching for shapes or design cues that transferred to the final 350Z. Creating a production car wasn't the object of the exercise at that point.

"We were not thinking of the final car, we were thinking of selling the program," Hirshberg points out, saying that the purpose of the initial model was to convince people "that we have tremendous credibility in some areas, and so the primary thing for us was to do a car that was a no-brainer Z, clearly a believable next Nissan Z if we were to have one."

Of course, the road show wasn't to be just a show for the press and analysts but was to boost morale and show those dispirited dealers there was light ahead—to have them say, "Yes, we can move that piece of metal . . . that's who we are!"

Even then, there were discussions of whether to do a forward-thinking Z or a retro design, but opinion tipped in favor of an identifiable Z, remembering that being

identifiably Nissan was critical. Getting into the heavy-duty discussion of retro versus forward-thinking would be addressed if they ever got assigned the project.

"So we did a contemporary, clean version, with elements of both the 300ZX and the 240Z," Hirshberg recalls. "It was a three-way argument. First, if you were going to do a retro car, which Z—the 300 or the 240? That was an interesting debate. The second one was, should it be retro at all? And the third one was, if not, what direction should the Z go?"

In just a few weeks, Vines was able to conjure up a budget for the concept car, and NDI was able to finish the design and transform the Z idea into a full-size model.

"It was terrific," Hirshberg enthuses. "The staff was wonderful—people like Tom Semple, Alfonso Albaisa, Diane Allen, and clay model experts Larry Brinker and Mark Short all jumped on the bandwagon. At that point word spread, and we were gaining some supporters along

the way. One by one, I was exposing the Z to people I thought would have the imagination to understand that even in this time of fear, it was not the time to be supercautious but time to take a bold stand. We were beginning to gain some support in sales and marketing. It was still highly questionable, but people were starting to run the numbers."

Besides dealers, the media attended some of these presentations . . . and the reaction to this car was powerful. NDI also had a Sport Utility Truck (SUT) concept clay and three future production cars in the show, but the Z car was the centerpiece.

"Jason was very much involved in a very positive way with the media, and some of the car magazines picked up the story. A number of people in the enthusiast media wrote, 'You guys have got to do this.' So there was hefty coverage, great excitement, and the letters started coming into the organization from all over."

After the dazzling success of the June 1998 Road-Show Z, the shape and detail of that car were refined for another show car, which was publicly displayed at the 1999 Detroit Auto Show.

Showing a retro flavor in a very smooth package, the 1999 Detroit Auto Show Z Concept got the public and the press revved up to the idea of the Z's return.

At one point, a top executive at Nissan told Hirshberg, "Jerry, you've done something very dangerous. You've put Nissan in a corner and made it very awkward for us to not do this car."

The designer smiles and says, "I actually did something very Japanese at that moment . . . I made a small inscrutable smile. Then I said, 'Guilty as charged. I want to back us into having to do something that we ought to be thrilled that we're doing.' The public and the media were suddenly turning positive, and that was at a time when there were running jokes about the organization. We used to kid that we should officially change our name to 'Nissan, the troubled corporation.' "

For the first time, there was talk about the Z inside Nissan—questions such as, "What chassis would it be on?" "What powerplant?" NDI made "some modestly clandestine approaches to the Japanese performance engineers. They are a great, great group of guys, who *really* know their stuff. We just floated this concept out to

them and asked if they would be willing to work with us in exploring the possibilities.

" 'Do you have any chassis?' 'What would the proportions be?' Even as we were doing the full-size model, we worked with our own very capable studio engineers. Guys like Bill Brown and Jeff Fusco were integrating our design with a viable chassis. But there was again no approval, nothing official about this."

Things got official after the successful road show, enough so that a running Z prototype was built for and shown at the 1999 Detroit Auto Show in January. Again the reception was dramatic and overwhelmingly in favor of the revival of the Z, enough so that at April's New York Auto Show, Nissan announced that the Z would live again.

Big Changes at Nissan

Then a major change took place. In March 1999, Renault bought its stake in Nissan, and Carlos Ghosn arrived on the scene. Would the Z pass his muster?

As part of taking on his duties as chief operating officer at Nissan, the highly regarded Ghosn made an international tour of all his key assets, including a stop at San Diego to visit NDI.

Hirshberg felt an instant rapport with Ghosn and says, "We saw in moments that we could speak frankly with him. He had heard about NDI and had come in with some positive feelings.

"I gave a spirited presentation on what we felt the problems were and what we wanted to do about it. I said during the report that with all the things we'd talked about—which were organizational and structural and a lot of other things, like throwing out the three-sedan strategy—I said that the number one priority, as trivial as this might sound, is I'd bring out the Z, and he said, 'Done.' Just like that. He had told me that the only Nissan he ever owned before taking this position was the Z, and he loved it."

It wasn't as simple as that, of course, because businessmen like Ghosn don't make expensive decisions off the cuff, but Hirshberg explains that he went on and "made this a challenge to the whole organization. Here were the conditions under which we would release this car: it must be profitable. It must come in under $30,000 . . . a very difficult assignment.

"What had happened is that up to this time, the vehicle was always killed because responsible-feeling [i.e., conservative] people at headquarters and at marketing in Los Angeles would say that they couldn't make the

Left: *The beautiful interior of the 1999 Z Concept showed little tie to the earlier Z cars, but offered nicely grouped gauges ahead of the driver as well as a satellite navigation system.*

Below: *Not just a pretty face, the 1999 Z Concept was finished as a running show car so onlookers could see what this new Z might look like on the road.*

Like all Z cars, the 1999 Detroit Show car was designed to be a very personal driver's car, with a cockpit created to make driving a sports car the pleasure it's meant to be.

The "eyes" of the 1999 Z Concept show a visual tie to the earliest Z cars, while the modular wheels and low-profile tires moved it into the 1990s.

numbers work out, that there weren't enough buyers to justify it.

"Carlos' feeling was that we were going to change those fundamental assumptions. We're not going to accept them as God-given—we're going to set ourselves goals, and we're going to achieve them. He did that across the board at Nissan, and to start it with a project like the Z was wonderful."

Hirshberg jumps ahead a bit and recalls how stunned even many of those in Nissan were when the 350Z's $26,600 base price was announced at the 2002 Detroit Auto Show. They had heard that the Z would come in under $30,000 and had hoped to see a price like $28,800, but to hear the final price, complete with a significant profit for Nissan and dealers, was "amazing." It was a prime example of how Ghosn had laid out goals for the new sports car and how successfully the new Nissan had met them.

Hirshberg goes on to say of Ghosn, "He had also committed to performance figures, saying that if we could not have this car perform as a bona fide, thoroughbred sports car, then we're not going to do it. So it was going to be done providing these financial and performance conditions were met, and those conditions were not stated as ifs, but 'This is how it will be.'

"We needed that kind of directness and clearheaded thinking and courage to go ahead and do it. Even then, it was challenging throughout the project, because at this point we were literally the little rowboat trying to turn around the entire organization, and some of this stuff was wired in . . . it had been there for so many generations.

"Also, this was a non-Japanese person calling the shots, and there was considerable inertia to overcome. But the forward momentum was palpable. And most of that momentum was due to Carlos, and a large chunk had to do with the charisma of the project itself. We weren't working on an unknown product. All we had to do was say the letter Z, and everybody knew what this meant.

"I guess my intuition from the beginning was that by tackling this car we would start remembering all the fundamental priorities and all the ways of acting, when winning was in our minds as opposed to merely avoiding failure."

A Real Project

So the Z became a real project and turned into a global design competition, because Ghosn saw it as a global car. Nissan's U.S., Japanese, and European studios got to work on the Z design and, Hirshberg says, "It was fun. I can honestly say that while each of the studios wanted to have its design selected, more than that everybody wanted a great car to win."

He echoes the comments of Diane Allen and Ajay Panchal, two NDI designers heavily involved in the production Z, when he explains that "the atmosphere was excellent, with designers doing sketches for 'the competition.' We shared our ideas and inspired each other . . . all we cared about was, 'Let's just make it a great automobile.' "

Many times, a final production design will grow from the sketches of several designers guided by a design chief,

but, Hirshberg points out, "This one really was penned by Ajay Panchal, such a wonderful, intelligent human being, and Diane is such a natural-born leader that between the two of them it was just delicious."

He then adds with a smile in his voice, "The devilish side of me enjoyed the fact a genuine sports-car design project was being led by a great designer who happened to be female and this Indian/British character . . . it was an unlikely team, but we looked at that sketch and it just flew off the wall into our faces. We thought, 'Wow, that's it!?' Under Diane, under Tom Semple, with Bruce Campbell, Alfonso Albaisa, and Larry Brinker, with me standing there beating the bass drum, it just got stronger and stronger."

Hirshberg recalls that during this time, NDI engineers were getting excited because their counterparts in Japan were really inspired. When the first test mule was sent to Nissan's Arizona test track, he had the chance to drive it.

"It scared me, and I thought, 'Wow, would this be street legal?' It was exciting, and we were asking, 'Can you guys actually do this for this money?' They were smiling and saying, 'Yes, we think we can.'

"The more important issue was, could we do a bona fide sports car that really was affordable for a broad cross-section of the public, a car that had genuine sports car characteristics? Our feeling was that some of the competition introduced after the death of the 300ZX, such as the entrants from Porsche and Mercedes and BMW and others, were vulnerable. Several of them were beautiful, but they were not thrilling in terms of performance. Therefore, to be able to come in with a sports car maybe half of what some of those cars cost, with a significantly better 0 to 60 time and high cornering speeds, etcetera, would really be something."

Which is exactly what Nissan managed to do—and yes, it is really something.

At the 1999 New York International Auto Show, Jerry Hirshberg (left), of Nissan Design International, was joined by Minoru Nakamura, president and CEO of Nissan (center) and the company's vice president and general manager, Michael Seergy, in announcing the Z car's return to production. **Nissan**

3
Defining the New Z

Creating a Soulful Machine (with a Profitable Heart)

Carlos Ghosn, the savior of Nissan, may have been a former 300ZX owner, but there was no way he would approve a new Z car without very good business arguments as to why he should. After all, it was a seemingly rational business decision that killed the 300ZX.

Joel Weeks, who heads product planning for the Z car, has been with Nissan for 15 years and explains the reasons but also the heartache that went with discontinuing the 300ZX. "When that car went away, it was like ripping our heart out as a company. We knew it was a great car, but it was expensive, and SUVs were becoming very popular. The hip new thing was to have an SUV. It gave you the sporty kind of feeling people wanted at that time. We think that's changing and this is a good time to introduce a sports car again.

"Our hearts told us we needed a Z car, but our minds and business sense said we couldn't do it. And to look at the numbers and the figures and the bottom line to redo a Z back then, especially in the company we had then, it was basically not feasible. The hard decision was made to not do another Z.

"They were hard times for us, very frustrating . . . the low depths of the company itself, not only losing the Z, but having some bland sedans. We'd had some good stuff, but they weren't refreshed."

Given the effect the loss of the Z had on Nissan, it's also an arguable business case that you can't *not* have your "halo" car around as a rallying point and showroom-traffic-increasing device. Weeks points out that this was well known in the company: "We knew we needed the flagship, the halo that was our spirit."

"In fact, our chief engineer, Mr. [Kazutoshi] Mizuno, had been working underground—off the books and off the record—trying to get the Z car back, working on a platform." Is such sub rosa work usual in Japanese company? "No, but I think that goes back to how strong the Z was for the company, how sad it was to see that car go away, and how many people wanted to see the right kind of Z come back."

Ah, but having "the right kind of Z" would be crucial to its return, and there was bound to be a difference of opinion about what was "right."

"Once we finally got the green light for the Z car," Weeks explains, "a really good internal discussion started."

As in other parts of the company, such as at Nissan Design International, there were long discussions about such things as doing a contemporary design versus a retro shape . . . and what is retro Z? A 240Z or a 300ZX? What size should the Z be? A small sports car? A big Grand Tourer? With a hatchback or trunk? Long hood, short deck?

To establish goals when planning the 350Z, Nissan engineers drove a variety of the world's best performance cars on many different types of roads.

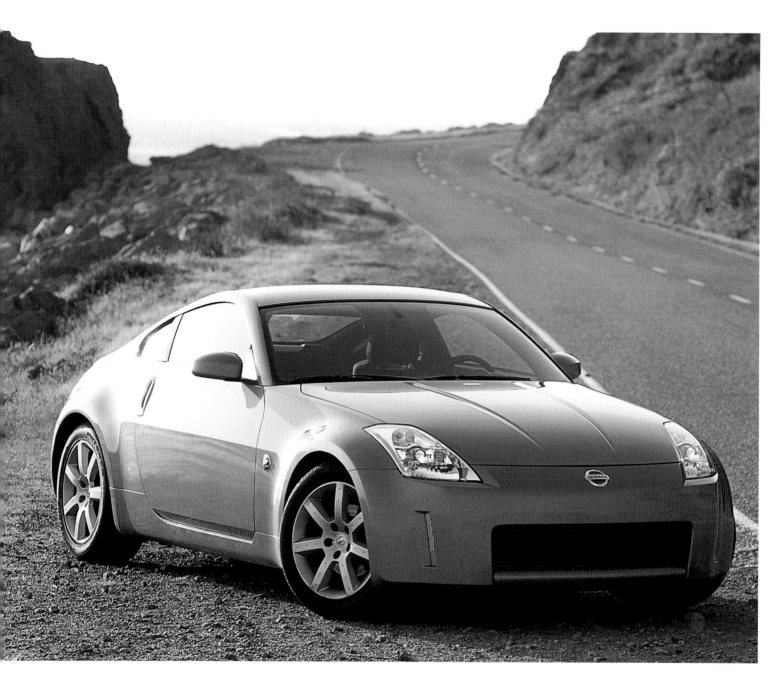

By 2002, some felt that the sport utility craze had peaked, and sports cars had a chance to score with the car-buying public, making cars like the 350Z more desirable.

"They were good discussions that went on, and I think the project does bring some reminiscence of the heritage of the old Z, with the longer hood and shorter rear profile, the three big gauges on the interior with a nod to the original car, but in a contemporary style that will live for quite a while."

In addition to establishing a theme for the new Z's character and exterior design, the Japanese and U.S. product planning and development teams had to set goals for the car's performance and handling. Nissan gathered what it thought were some of the best sports automobiles

in the world to establish benchmarks for the new Z car. Included in the group was Nissan's own Skyline GTR (a 4-wheel drive legend in Japan), an Acura NSX, a Chevrolet Corvette, a Porsche Boxster, a BMW M3 coupe and, on the bottom end, a Mitsubishi Eclipse.

"About 10 people from Nissan took those cars on several road trips around the U.S.," Weeks relates. "They went up toward Monterey, drove mountain roads around Los Angeles, did some work in the Phoenix area, and got a consensus. Which in the group of cars were the best in performance, handling, 0 to 60 mph times? Certain cars

fell off the map. Eclipse was too much a sporty coupe, Skyline was maybe too brawny, too much performance, and the Corvette was almost the same way . . . not really what they called a 'dance partner.'

"So we took a little bit of what the Boxster had to offer, a bit of the M3, and aspects of certain cars we thought, from a concept, best fit what the new Z should be."

Eventually, engineers tested for actual data—0 to 60 mph times, lateral acceleration, and so forth—and targets were developed, such as a 0 to 60 time of under 6.0 seconds. As the new Z car moved forward, it needed to meet those targets before it could be released for production.

"If I could take one of those cars and pull it out, probably the Boxster would be closest to what we wanted to try to be. . . . That car would be included in all our meetings as we checked against it."

An interesting choice, given that the Porsche is a mid-engine car, but Weeks continues, "We liked a lot of what the Boxster delivered in performance and handling, though again we took some things from other cars, too." As an example, a Honda S2000 has one of the best-shifting manual transmissions in the world. Nissan couldn't quite duplicate it because of the Z's V-6 torque, but it was the bogie.

With the rebirth of the Z car, Nissan was able to recapture its corporate soul, one it had given up in response to flagging mid-1990s sales of the 300ZX.

Although many drivers love the romance of a sports car, in the 1990s the rise of the sport utility vehicle turned many consumers away from smaller automobiles.

Talking to Owners

In addition to all this internally developed data, research into what the Z should be involved talking with an important ingredient in any sports car program: people who already own them. Like any great sports car, the Datsun and Nissan Z cars have active, ardent owner's clubs, so members were asked what they thought about a new Z.

The reactions were not unexpected. Weeks recalls, "Some of the groups we talked to said they wouldn't consider this car. They included the type of person who goes out every weekend to tweak the carburetors or

whatever and here comes this 2003 350Z, a highly technical Z car on which you can't do much other than wash it.

"But what also bubbled up was this intense love for Z cars." They found there were owners who, even though they can't work on the carbs, figured it's a Z car and I love it and if I don't buy it myself, I'm going to tell my next-door neighbor to get one.

"It was a love-hate thing for some of them, and I think it has actually turned around. Since the car has come out and gotten some really good press—plus the fact it's a damn good car—some of the people who might have

One of the target cars for Nissan engineers who developed the 350Z was Honda's highly regarded S2000, a car with a front-mounted, four-cylinder engine that manages to produce 240 horsepower from just 2.0 liters of displacement.

Perhaps the major bogie for the 350Z is Porsche's Boxster, which has its engine located just behind the passenger compartment. The Boxster is respected for its style, power, and handling.

been doubters are actually buying them. They can tweak their early Z car, but they can drive their 350Z all day long and not worry about it."

Among the specific issues Nissan wanted to discuss with the clubs was the need for a hatchback design. "With the high handling targets we had," Weeks explains, "engineering said there was no way to do a hatchback, that this was not the way to go." The problem was the overall rigidity of the body, which should be high to provide a stable platform, so the suspension can best do its work. The problem is that a hatchback requires a big hole in the body for the hatch, making it difficult to achieve the high level of rigidity you could in a design with a trunk.

"We thought hard about how a hatchback design helps you on a daily basis," Weeks continues. "You can put

the groceries in, luggage is easy to store, so we fought hard in combination with the input from the clubs to convince engineering to put a little more weight and structure in the car and take some weight out somewhere else."

Which the engineers did, though they also installed the brace that runs across the rear luggage area connecting the tops of the rear suspension struts (a similar brace ties the front suspension struts together). It's a practical engineering solution, but it creates an obstruction across the luggage area. Weeks says they have encountered reactions against the brace "and shown how you can get quite a bit of luggage in there. Two golf bags . . . and once you tell people the brace was done to meet the handling targets, objections kind of go away."

Market research tends to be an integral part of every new car, though it is used with varying degrees from one

car company to the next. "We did one clinic, and that's one change that's happened since Renault has come. The French are trying to basically instill in us that we should be confident in our designs for concepts . . . try to find a nice balance of professional judgment, new great ideas, and bring some research in, but once you do that, don't totally make or break a design based on research."

As Nissan defined the new Z car, as the design evolved and was then "frozen," and as engineering development continued, hundreds of practical decisions had to be made, to meet goals set for such things as performance and profit. Planners had a general concept for the car they labeled "Lust, then love," and as they moved forward, that theme started evolving in bits and pieces, into development work, into a truer vehicle. Budget, profit, and cost issues arose, balancing tradeoffs . . . if you spend so much money on the engine to meet a target for performance, how much do you have to spend on the interior?

"People have hammered us at times about the fender-mounted antenna," Weeks points out. "Why didn't we use either a power antenna or an antenna in the glass? Because there was a decision to spend money on performance instead of doing an expensive power antenna or a glass antenna . . . a typical tradeoff. The difference in price can be twenty dollars per car, but we even argue about things that cost four or five cents."

And it makes a difference, because a relatively low price is arguably as important an element of Z history as its powerful engine and tempting styling.

"We were lucky," Joel Weeks comments. "We looked back at our history, and one of the main goals of the 350Z was to reinvent what the 240Z did. We were fortunate that the market dynamics today are much like those in the late 1960s and early 1970s.

"If you look at a comparison of performance cars and their prices versus lower-end cars, there's a gap between them." He points out that the new crop of sports cars since the decline of the 300ZX—Porsche Boxster, Audi TT, BMW Z3 and now Z4, Honda S2000—tend to have out-the-door prices that start in the mid-$30,000 to $40,000 range and can easily take a buyer up to $50,000.

In early 2003 Nissan released the first photos of the Roadster version. In summer 2003, one year after the 350Z went on sale, the Roadster version was released. Designed at the same time as the coupe, which was created in the traditional clay-model manner, the Roadster was developed using computers. With a soft folding top that collapses behind the seats and stows beneath a hard tonneau cover, the car looks quite handsome with the top down or up. Nissan

Next step down is the area with the Mazda Miata and Mitsubishi Eclipse. Weeks explains, "You'll find 'white space' between them that was totally open . . . sub-$30,000, delivering 0 to 60 mph performance under 6.0 seconds, horsepower figures close to 300, with great handling.

"Go back to 1969 and 1970 and you had Porsche 911s and Corvettes in one area, and the 240Z came in under them. Move the timeframe ahead and we think we're mimicking the success we had back then, filling a space where no other car lives, delivering great value. As I believe Mr. Ghosn explained it, 'Fifty-thousand-dollar sports car performance for under thirty thousand dollars.' "

As interesting as the prices is the way Nissan packaged the cars into five different models. Weeks said, "After looking at some research work about what the competition is doing and not doing . . . well, I love Porsches, but they are so complex when it comes to ordering options. We also have goals internally as we get better as a company, to slim down our complexity."

This matter of complexity is an important issue on many levels. For the customer, a too-long option list can be daunting, a confusion that carries over to the company as many individualized orders are passed along through a system dealing with tens of thousands of cars. At the factory, a huge number of options, colors, interior fabrics, and such hinders quality control as it dramatically ups the chances for error.

Besides, Weeks adds, "Say a customer wanted a Z with package A in a red color and there were so many iterations because of options that he couldn't get it, so another dealer had to ship it to a local dealer and it cost an extra $200 . . . it adds to customer frustration."

The main frustration for both sides was going to be getting enough Z cars in customers' hands as quickly as possible. But after its recent history, the frustrations of dealing with a hot-selling car like the 350Z was something Nissan could look forward to.

The standard 350Z is just $26,269, complete with the basic package, 287 bhp V-6, 6-speed manual transmission, independent suspension with 17-inch wheels, sub-6.0 seconds to 60 mph, and that sensational styling.

Next come the Enthusiast Model versions, $28,249 with a 6-speed or $29,219 with the 5-speed automatic transmission, and such important extras as the viscous limited-slip differential, cruise control, traction control, and xenon headlights.

The Performance Model at $30,429 starts with the Enthusiast equipment and adds 18-inch wheels, the tire-pressure warning system, and an electronic wonder for the suspension, Vehicle Dynamic Control (VDC).

There are two Touring Models, the automatic transmission version at $31,589 adding more luxury, like the heated, power-adjustable, leather-"appointed" seats—the other models get seats covered with "carbon cloth"—and a 240-watt Bose sound system. Opt for the $33,179 6-speed manual edition and you get all that plus the 18-inch wheels and VDC.

Most Z performance, however, comes from the Track Model, which removes the luxo touring equipment such as the Bose sound system and goes for lighter weight, plus VDC, front and rear spoilers, 18-inch wheels used only on this model and, lurking inside them, big Italian Brembo disc brakes . . . at $34,079.

Nissan even developed a strategy to keep overcharging by its dealers to a minimum. Pricing was announced six months before the cars were being delivered from Japan, and a website allowed customers to go online, configure their cars, and be aware of prices. Information was passed back and forth online between potential Z owners, and word got out about which dealers were keeping prices to a reasonable level and which weren't. Weeks figures that "for the presale program, 85–90 percent of those 8,000 cars went out the door at the sticker price."

There's even a story going around the Internet about dealers who got calls from high-level Nissan executives asking them to "rethink your pricing strategy" on the Z, followed by calls from those dealers to Z buyers, who were told the dealer had redone paperwork on the car and was now charging $3,000 less.

It can't hurt, of course, that Nissan dealers should feel better about their products and prospects than they have in more than a decade. The Z is just one of many new Nissan products on their showroom floors, from the new Maxima sedan to the Murano SUV.

And another new Z. Just six months after putting the 350Z on the market, Nissan followed up with the open-air version of the sports car. Called the 350Z Roadster, it looks as good as the coupe, something that could not be said of the 300ZX ragtop. Fitted with a power-operated soft folding top with a glass rear window, the Roadster was debuted at the 2003 New York Auto Show, to go on sale beginning summer 2003. Price? In the range of $28,000.

Makes you wonder about the future of the 350Z, and naturally Joel Weeks won't discuss what's coming, but there is this reality: "Even with a great design like we have, we think we're looking at a peak for this sports car design . . . maybe two to three years of great sales, but being honest from a business standpoint, letting the volume drop off a bit towards the end until we refresh the car again. We are planning a good mid-lifecycle, throw in some horsepower, whether it's a normally aspirated increase or even some forced induction. But we are making sure—looking at the past, what Porsche and BMW have done with their sports cars—that we keep them fresh to try as best as possible to keep the volume up."

So, what do you suppose they have in mind?

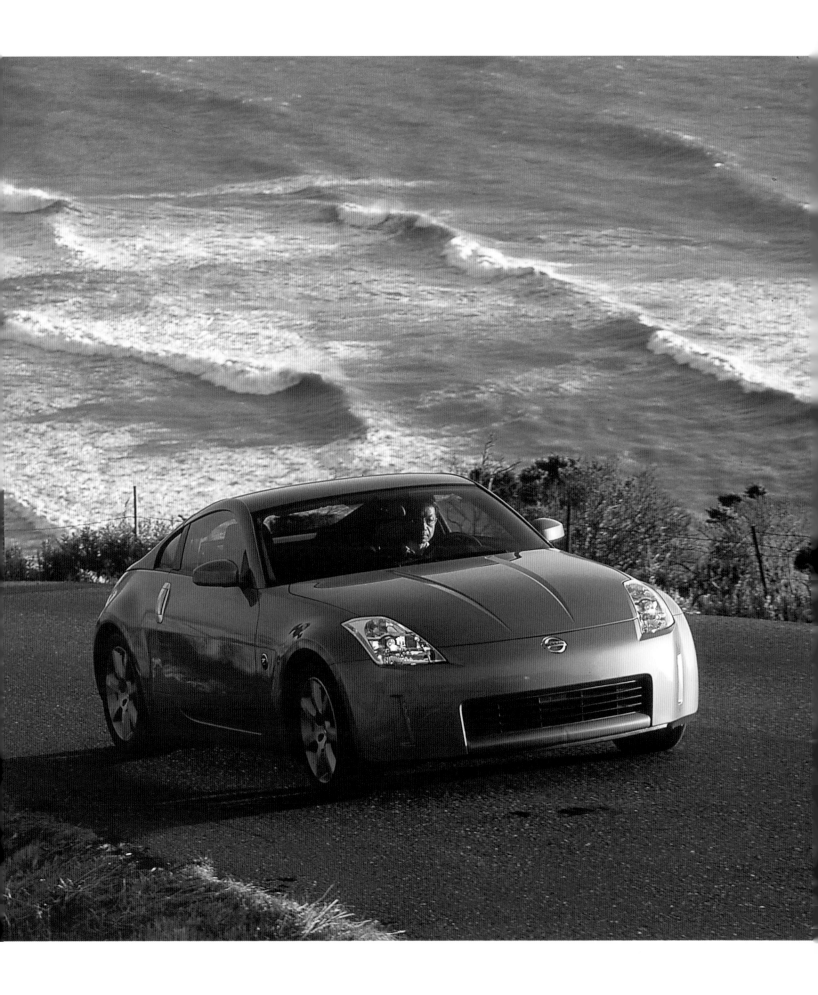

4

A Modern Retro Design

Shaping Clay with Z DNA

Diane Allen has been with Nissan for 19 years, ever since she graduated from Detroit's Center for Creative Studies. Though not from an automotive family, the native of Motown participated in the revival of the Z as head of Nissan Design America's "Red Studio," where the production car was created, but she points out that the 1998 concept car "was birthed by the passion of designers like Jerry Hirshberg. He just thought the Z had to come back. This was well before the French got involved, but Jerry just loved the idea of the Z, and he went ahead with his own program to propose a Z, to say we're alive. It was more of a temperature reading to see if people were excited to see the Z again."

At Detroit's 1999 North American International Auto Show, the public got its first look at the Z proposal. Like most such concept cars, it had its lovers and detractors, but the one message that came through from everyone was that it was great to have the Z car—or at least the prospect of one—back on the radar screen.

"Love or hate the design," Allen continues, "it got people talking and put the Z back into discussions in the boardroom. The reception of that proposal pretty much put it right on the sheet for what we call a 'square b plan,' which is production, and they decided to put it back into

our lineup." Allen adds that Carlos Ghosn "knew that it was important for Nissan to show its success by showing our heritage and bringing back the car."

Now came the tough part. While there was little argument that Z should return, opinions were many and varied about what form that Z should take.

As the advanced phase of design began in early 1999, Allen recalls, "We did a ton of designs, and what we were doing was playing with proportion, working on 'What is Z-ness?' and all these things. It was definitely going to be front-engine, rear-drive . . . we did not want a midship-looking car, we wanted it to definitely look like our heritage."

That heritage dictated that the new Z have a hatchback. "We didn't want to do a trunk style of car," Allen explains. "During the six months we worked on the advanced stage, we brought up the important aspects of what we were going to be and what we weren't going to be. The one thing we started to hit on was this idea that it should be a wheel-oriented design, kind of fuselage-shaped, and that's what set it in motion." Overlaying all this was one important question: "Jerry's car opened the discussion over whether we should do a retro car or visionary future. That was a great, rich debate."

One of the defining images of the new 350Z is how it sits so confidently on the road, thanks to its proportions and also the manner in which the wheels and tires nicely fill the wheelwells.

It was decided that the Z should be a wheel-oriented design, which you can see here with its beautiful fender flares.

Retro or Visionary Look?

Remember that this was the time of retro designs, led by Volkswagen's new Beetle, Chrysler's PT Cruiser, BMW's Mini, Ford's resurrected two-person Thunderbird, and, to an extent, Audi's TT.

"It seemed there were love affairs with the original 240Z and the last 300ZX, and what we were discovering was that there was not only an argument about going retro or future, but the pro-retro people weren't in sync with each other, some loving the 240Z and some the

300ZX. We always thought everyone arguing retro was behind the 240Z, but when we heard Carlos Ghosn, he was in love with the 300ZX.

"So the debate was all over the map. But as we really considered where Nissan was going, we understood that what we wanted to do was put out a vehicle that showed our future and not just celebrate our past. We needed to put a foot in the future, to show we are right on track again, and that's what I think won out the debate for doing a visionary Z-car design, not one that just paid homage to the past.

A lovely bit of design, the 350Z's headlamps are just one of the many details that had to be finalized during the months when the car's design was refined in Nissan's Japanese studios.

"Nissan changed quite dramatically when Carlos Ghosn came onboard, and the direction was definitely more progressive. When the 240Z came out, it was a pretty modern design, and when the 300ZX came out, it was, for its time, a modern design—so why should this Z not be modern for its time? That was our argument for pushing for a more progressive design."

"There was also the fact we were able to do a Z for the twenty-first century in the first year of the century," chimes in Ajay Panchal, the young British-born designer who gets credit for penning the final shape of the new Z car.

"It was a bit of a battle, even amongst designers . . . an enjoyable one at that, with people doing retro and futuristic models. I think as designers we really had to question ourselves."

There was also another argument against a heavy retro design. While retro designs are greeted with great warmth, enthusiasm, and strong initial sales, their long-term sales potential is questionable. They seem to quickly peak in sales and then taper off to a steady but modest level (as do many new sports cars). Once the sales of those who just couldn't wait to get one are satisfied, the appeal declines.

Allen underlines their concern about this problem when she explains, "We're in for the long haul, and this design was about a statement for the long haul. I think there is a lifespan to the retro look . . . seen it, done it, been there. We wanted to challenge people, though at the same time embrace the beauty of Z. So then, once we decided, okay, this is going to be a visionary program, then it got really interesting as to how do you capture 'Nissan-ness'?"

To do this, the designers created a chart that contained such aspects as design quality and design newness to graphically display the potential aspects of the new Z. And naturally, that led to more new questions. Allen mentions one: "It had to be new, but then there was the interesting point made that if it's new, is it all about newness, or is it a balance of timelessness with new? Sometimes if you go too modern you're not timeless, and we had to make sure this thing had a beauty quotient that meant, for instance, that for years to come you'd want to wax it by hand."

Panchal adds that while newness is important, "how are people going to recognize it as a Z? We came upon the term 'Z DNA' and used that phrase a lot. So we set up the chart with 240 on the left and 300 on the right, to

1999 Design Sketches

These 1999 sketches, when Nissan's studios in the United States, Japan, and Europe laid out proposals for the upcoming Z, show a turn away from retro and a lean toward a forward-looking shape. **Nissan**

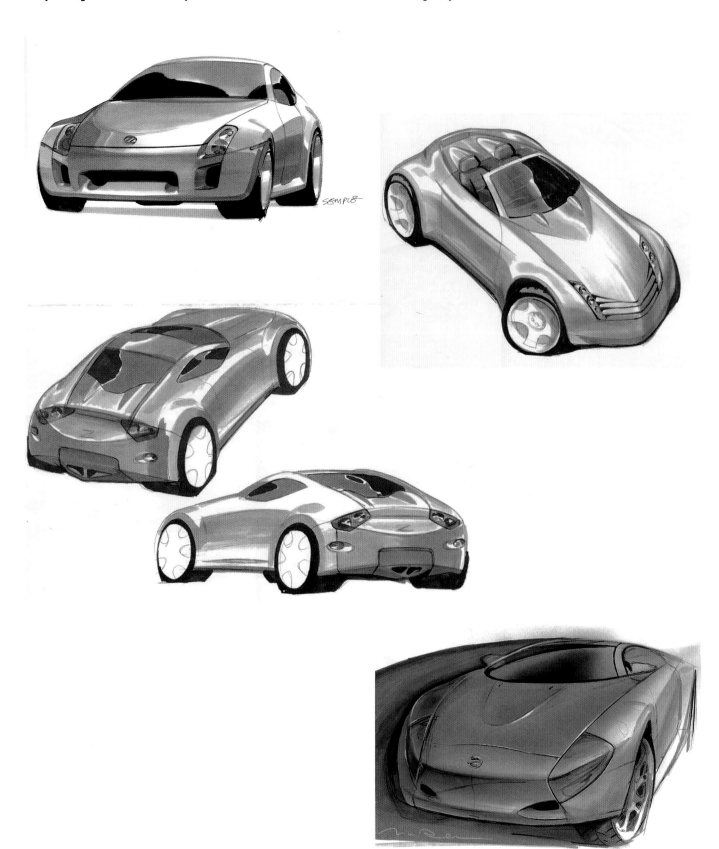

1999 Design Sketches (continued)

SEE THROUGH MATERIAL

Ajay Panchal created this sketch, which was the inspiration for the final Z-car design. Note the slight concave section just below the beltline and how the door handle arcs over it. **Nissan**

Tom Semple, who now heads Nissan Design America, is the one person who followed the 350Z from the early discussions about a new Z car in 1998 through to the design process in the United States and then Japan, where it was painstakingly taken to production. Nissan really address the aspects of both of these cars . . . capture the whole generation of cars."

Allen points out, "We wanted to capture the good parts and get rid of the bad parts but do it in a way that wasn't copying but taking the essence, the thought behind what made these cars great. With 240, that meant fun to drive, light and agile, industrial chic, high testosterone." She continues, "There was a fun factor here . . . true sports, selfish cockpit, that kind of thing." That was the good side of the first Z car, but there was a downside too: the car was "thin-walled, a derivative of another sports car, and it was a little on the crude side."

Panchal covers the 300ZX's good points, calling the car, "a little more upscale, more polished, beautiful, but the downside was that maybe it was a little too sweet to be a pure sports car or maybe a bit too luxurious when you look at traditional sports cars. It did have some purity, and we wanted to recapture the essence of that. The other question was, should we do a GT or a pure sports car? For a lot of us, the 300ZX was a GT and the 240Z was a sports car. We wanted to capture a lot more of the sports car feeling."

A Visual Distilling Process

During this period, many designers at NDA were doing sketches that might become the new Z car, as were designers at Nissan's advanced studios in Japan and Europe. This is something of a visual distilling process, with certain designs surviving the boiling-off process to be made into clay models. From July to October 1999, the studios were in the advanced design stages, not just refining shapes but also working with engineers to make certain that whatever they created would fit over the proposed technical package of chassis and driveline.

From these ideas and clay models, certain themes came through. Diane Allen, for example, had done an exciting design establishing that the team liked the sense of a fuselage shape with a strong wheel orientation, a smaller cockpit, and a good dashboard-to-front-axle distance that announced the front-engine nature of the car.

Come October, Carlos Ghosn put the official stamp of approval on production of the Z car at the Tokyo Motor

Show, moving design into a new stage. All the designs done in California, Japan, and Europe were reviewed and the possibilities honed down. The European studio was removed from the picture, having been assigned another important new project. Shapes that had survived the sifting and winnowing process at NDA would now be transformed into full-size clays to compete against the proposals from the studio in Japan.

A short delay followed. They stopped the project because as the car got more and more engineering input, it began to vary from the "package" they were originally given. It wasn't a sports car anymore, but a sports coupe.

They put the brakes on. It was back to the drawing board to negotiate things like windshield touchdown (where it meets the body) and A-pillar position. Then they restarted the production program.

What they mean by a "package" is the physical dimensions the designers are given to work around, such as the wheelbase length of the platform on which the car will be built, front and rear overhangs, and the physical dimensions of the drivetrain, suspension, fuel tank, steering, and so on that must be contained within the body shape. The "package" also includes the practical size of the interior, dashboard structure, where the occupants will sit, and where their luggage can be stored. Engineers know exactly how much room is needed for all this, and designers known exactly how they want the car to look. At times, these goals conflict, and the two sides negotiate and accommodate.

Allen explains, "Because we were really sharing this same package with the Infiniti G35, there was a lot of negotiation going on, where we as designers fought, for example, for an A-pillar [the windshield pillar] that was back and inboard, in order for it to have tumbleover and for the wheels to be the farthest point out. Through design, we made a case for a lot of the engineering moves in which they invested and helped us to achieve our goals."

This is when the designers and engineers really earn their money. The designers are trying to maintain, for instance, the purity of a line that stretches from nose to tail, while the engineers are concerned about the height of a suspension strut tower. Allen points out, "When you move even one or two millimeters, it changes the essence of the line, but I have to give credit to the people who made the final production clays for honoring what we wanted to achieve."

The Program Resumes

After the short delay, the program was again at full speed. The designers knew the direction they wanted to go with the new Z but were still looking for that final version, so between October and January 5, 2000, Allen says with a smile, "We did a whole bunch of new scale models, and everybody in the building participated. But Ajay's design kept standing out as being this future-visionary tension. It was wheel-oriented, everything we wanted it to be. But there was even conflict about the fact it was too far out there, not Nissan enough—how do we make it more Nissan? Everyone was so passionate about the project."

That January 5, 2000, date was when the field was trimmed to two. A meeting in Japan pitted two NDA designs—Panchal's and one that was more retro—against four from Nissan's home studio. Panchal's was chosen, along with one of the latter.

Allen recounts, "Overwhelmingly, the design managers picked Ajay's. They just said, 'Make it look more Nissan.' And that was our job as we went into the production phase, which started as soon as we could get the models back to the U.S."

What with shipping the clays back to the U.S., it was coming up on February before they could begin this last production phase of design. Time would be tight, because the final, full-size clay had to be shipped to Japan in mid-March for the final contest between the two proposals.

Allen, who has been through many design programs in her 19 years with the company, interjects that all this was made easier because "There was a wonderful new mood at Nissan. It was no longer us against them"—a studio-against-studio confrontation that is not unusual within many automakers, each studio protecting its turf. "We had to survive our financial problems, get it together, and work as one team."

This new feeling of openness meant that the U.S. and Japanese studios shared digital images of each other's cars and knew what the other was doing. Formerly, they wouldn't have had a clue what the other studio's design looked like until they walked into the room where the final decision was about to be made.

"They used to think it was healthy to not see each other's models, but this time they were visiting us, we were seeing their products, and it was great," Allen explains.

The car that Panchal and the studio refined during that month and a half is surprisingly close to what we see on the streets today. In fact, the concept car shown at the 2000 North American International Auto Show in Detroit the next January was taken directly from this clay and was only slightly changed to create the final production 350Z.

The studio lights burned late as the Nissan team in San Diego beavered away at the final design for the big decision day in Japan. Daylight had its advantages too, as Panchal points out: "We only had six or seven weeks to do the car, and we'd take the clay model outside. Modelers would bring clay, and we'd adjust things outdoors, because we knew it was important that this car look good there too, not just in the studio."

He explains, "Being outside is so different than being in the studio. For one thing, you can get away from the design and see it from a distance. A big part of our feeling was this car had to capture emotion, and we couldn't do that in the studio . . . and it seemed that every time we went outside, we learned something new."

Clay, Not Computers

What wasn't new was the technique employed to create the new Z car. Many of today's new cars are increasing being designed inside and out on computers. Using a program called Alias, designers are able to package and design entire new cars in the computer.

Possibly the best example to date is Volvo's hot-selling XC90 sport utility, which was designed on computers in the company's Camarillo, California, studio. The only full-size models were early design suggestions cut from high-density foam under a computer's

1999 Nissan Design America Scale Models

Intriguing scale models from mid-1999, created at Nissan Design America, highlight the search for the appropriate Z shape. Nissan

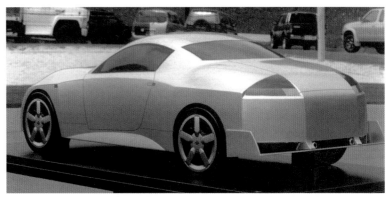

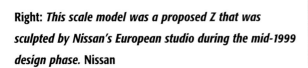

Right: *This scale model was a proposed Z that was sculpted by Nissan's European studio during the mid-1999 design phase.* Nissan

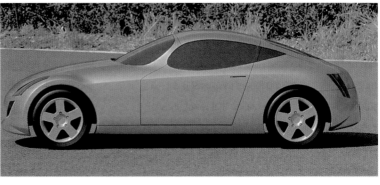

direction. Just one clay model was created, in the final stages of design.

It's fascinating to watch the process, the car essentially a multitude of data bits on a screen or—and this is amazing—a full-size screen or 3D projection you swear you could reach out and touch.

Fascinating, but the NDA studio stuck with tradition in developing the 350Z, working closely with clay modelers. Going from sketches to small-scale clay models and then to full-size clays, the designers interact closely with the modelers, who are doing much more than just shaping and finishing the models to reflect the design drawings. Highly skilled, the modelers as a group add their own signatures to the design and are an integral part of the final product.

Not that computers were ignored. Allen explains that the convertible version of the new 350Z was developed on the computer using Alias, "which was really the first time we used that program for design. So when we went to the final show, we had our full-size model all finished, with the lights working by remote control, and we also had images of our convertible to show that the car could work well as both an open and closed design."

In early April, the clay was in Japan with a good-sized deputation from NDA. Probably the most nervous was Panchal, who admits to getting little sleep the night before the big decision. "I was very excited. It was obviously a huge day in my life. The meeting was at Nissan's Atsugi headquarters, in one of the studios where clays are done. You had to walk in through curtains, because of security, and as you entered the room, we had our model first, and theirs was behind. They set up spotlights to highlight the beauty aspects of each car, and behind them were two walls, where we put images that might communicate design aspects.

"Carlos Ghosn was there, as were all the studio chiefs, and what I love with the new Nissan is how democratic they were about the process. Clearly Carlos Ghosn and Shiro Nakamura (Nissan's design chief) have the major say in design direction, but they actually asked everybody what they thought, and the chief designers then took a vote on which car they favored. There were about thirteen or fourteen managers, and all but maybe one

voted for ours. To go to Japan and see that reaction from the Japanese was wonderful.

"It was an amazing moment . . . we were all very happy and excited."

Hundreds of Small Issues

And now that the final design of the new Z had been chosen, other issues had to be dealt with. Panchal would spend two months in Japan, helping with the final details. Studio head Tom Semple would devote a half year in Japan to the 350Z. This made him one of the true 350Z heroes, the one person from NDI and then NDA who was with the car from Jerry Hirshberg's first discussions in 1998 until the day the car went into production. Several people from the San Diego studio would be involved after this, but most of the work fell to the studio in Japan, and it is unglamorous, difficult work.

Hundreds of small issues had to be dealt with in transforming the Z into production, such as avoiding interference fits between body and internal components. What happens when the engineers need a suspension strut to move a few millimeters, which would take it into the sheetmetal? How will the windows drop into the doors properly? Ever try to integrate windshield wipers or door hinges into an automotive design? And then you have to make sure the car is easy to assemble.

As with any new car, there were aerodynamic issues, so they put a one-quarter-scale model in a wind tunnel in Osaka. "We learned a great deal," Panchal says. "Aerodynamically, the car needed some improvements. The engineers argued for a very stable platform, and they lifted the tail up to add stability, which also helped the aero numbers."

All this work was going on about the same time Audi's TT was coming under scrutiny (and adding a rear spoiler) because its back end sloped too quickly, causing rear-end lift and a few accidents. The net result for the 350Z was a prudent 60 mm increase in the height of the tail.

Panchal adds, "They anticipated that the fuselage shape with the prominent fenders might not do that well in the tunnel, but the coefficient of drag that came back wasn't bad once they fixed the tail."

One major, interesting change was the nose. The car shipped to Japan had a split front grille, with an intake on each side of the front. Panchal's original small clay model had a full-width grille up front, with what he calls a small "tooth" in the middle. This was changed to the twin-intake design, for the sake of distinctiveness.

In the end, both were scrapped in favor of a rectangular, full-width grille, for several reasons. The twin-intake grille had a slight Porsche feel to it. The larger, single grille not only conveyed a feeling of Nissan's heritage but also eased some cooling issues with the radiators.

Other changes that might seem small involved hours of concentrated work by the designers. You can see some of it in the differences between the near-final shape of the Detroit 2000 concept Z and today's production car. For instance, the grille size was adjusted after criticism that it was too big on the show car. The headlights were made less triangular and more square,

echoing the front of the 300ZX and making them a little less like the Toyota Celica's.

This work was overseen by the man in charge of all design, Shiro Nakamura, working with Tsunehiro Kunimoto, the general manager of passenger cars, and Toshio Yamashita, the first chief designer, with the responsibility later transferred to Mamoru Aoki. Diane Allen, talking about all the work that had to be done in Japan to ready the 350Z for production says, "Most people have no idea of what a *big job* that is."

When the definitive production 350Z finally began showing up on the public roads in mid-2002, there was no denying that all those hours in San Diego and Atsugi had been well spent. It causes drivers to follow the new Z, to give it the once-, twice-, even three-times over. It has brought to Nissan dealers prospective buyers who hadn't been there in years . . . if ever.

The 350Z's design was created at Nissan Design America in La Jolla, California, near San Diego, and then refined into production form in Nissan's Japan studio.

1999 Japanese Nissan Studio Designs

Nissan's studio in Japan presented these 350Z design suggestions in mid-1999. Note the various approaches to the glass area in the greenhouse portion of the models. Nissan

How Do the Designers Describe the 350Z's Exterior?

Diane Allen describes the Z's design as "the marriage of form with crisp intersections and really super-powerful tension in the lines, adding real modern detailing." She adds, "We always thought it would be great if a child could draw this with just a few lines. That's what we were shooting for. For me, the way the light hits some of these forms yet the way it's defining itself with edges and crispness here and there . . . that's what I think is the beauty of the modern and yet timeless part of the 350Z."

Ajay Panchal explains, "We came to call the design theme a 'fusion of contrasts'—how we mixed positive wheel forms against hollow sections, very sexy highlights against mechanical details . . . it's a juxtaposition throughout the whole car, an interplay between shapes and feelings. Often when you see a car, it's either all edgy or all soft. I think this is the first car in a long time that's kind of a marriage of these two looks. To me, that's where it feels new but constantly enticing."

"To me it's like a 3D moving sculpture. You can't get bored with it—you kind of tend to walk around the car. The way the light falls on the shape changes with each angle. It's very sculptural, and I think that goes back to both Diane and my backgrounds, which are more artistic.

"We came to coin a phrase for the look or feeling we were after when we were trying to explain to the modelers: to 'think of it like liquid metal.' We want you to think of the form as a mechanical structure underneath and then imagine a sheet of liquid metal just draped and falling very naturally over all the parts of the car."

In addition to the fuselage shape with the distinctive wheel arches at each end of the 350Z, it's also important to recognize the importance of the beltline that runs from front to rear. Allen points out how the front and rear lights act as "anchors" for the beltline and "gave reason for it to be there. If it was just floating there, I think it wouldn't be as powerful as it is . . . and the way it is anchored at each end with these very iconic, technological shapes was, for us, part of that simple, child-could-draw-it thinking.

"All the Zs of the past were simple. They're not overdone . . . but have simple confidence. We wanted to maintain that, but with a modern graphic." Panchal adds, "Generally, we tried to do that with all the details, to give the feeling they're part of the car and they've been designed as a key feature rather than adding extraneous elements."

The comment begs us to ask about the new Z car's most distinctive detail, its door handles. First, you must note that just below the beltline of the Z car is a slight hollow section, a bit of indentation. Panchal explains, "The door handle was originally meant as a contrast to the hollow section. It was a play on these hollow details, almost emphasizing them with the way its shadow would make them even stronger.

"The other feeling was emotional . . . so when you walk up to the car it would have a sense of occasion, and anything you touch or feel would have a tactile response. To me, sometimes a door handle is an afterthought on a car, and with this it's an occasion you're not going to forget. It's very unique, no other car has a door handle like this . . . you will not forget it. Some people who have driven the car say it invites you to open the door and get in . . . like an invitation . . . and that was the goal."

1999 Clay Models by Nissan U.S. Designer Diane Allen

October 1999 saw Nissan's various studios displaying full-size clay models to represent their ideas of what the new Z should look like. This one was created by Diane Allen, of the U.S. studio. **Nissan**

1999 Japanese Nissan Design Studio Full-Size Model

Japanese designers for Nissan made this full-size model, which carries a drooping glass area. Nissan

1999 European Nissan Design Studio Full-Size Model

Nissan Design Europe had this full-scale interpretation of what a Z should be. After these late-1999 designs, this team was given a new assignment and the field was honed down to the U.S. and Japanese studios. Nissan

Ajay Panchal: It's a Long Way from Leicester, England, to La Jolla, California

Ajay Panchal must have a very understanding mother. The designer of the 350Z recalls, "I started at a very young age drawing cars on the wallpaper . . . anywhere there was paper, I would draw cars."

Panchal, born in Leicester, England, inherited his passion for automobiles from his auto mechanic dad and earned an automotive design degree from Coventry University. Hired by Ford's Dunton studio, the young designer was slated to start his master's degree at the Royal College of Art when he won the transport design category in a Royal Society of Arts contest.

The prize? A trip to a place of his liking, so he booked a ticket to California, where automakers from Volkswagen to BMW to Toyota maintain design studios. Before beginning his advanced studies, he wanted to check in with the many design studios and keep his name in the loop. His second stop was Nissan Design International.

Not only is San Diego reputed to have the best weather in the U.S., but Panchal like the fact that at NDI, "The people are wonderful. It's a very human studio. People coming to the meeting in shorts, so casual, the sort of place you don't want to leave." He also liked the ultramodern building that houses the studios.

When he returned for a second interview the same day, his fate was sealed. Offered a job on the spot, Panchal signed a contract and then called home and roused his parents in England at 3 A.M. to tell them he was making the move to California.

Panchal liked the idea of the extensive car culture in California, but explains that when he signed on with Nissan, "It was clear that Nissan was a company that had done great work in the past but at that time wasn't quite sure which direction to take. So do you go to a company that establishes design directions or one that doesn't? Nissan does, and for someone like me, who likes to start with themes and big-picture designs, the opportunity to come to this kind of company was better.

"It has worked so well with Renault and Nissan," he continues, "and with Carlos Ghosn. In the past, we've done great designs, but they got lost in the system. Carlos Ghosn and Shiro Nakamura spot things they like, and they tend to find a way to develop the projects. I love that passion and human side of projects."

Asked about his favorite cars of all time, the 30-year-old designer goes Italian, naming classics like Alfa Romeo's Disco Volante and Ferrari's 250GTO. He saves special mention, however, for a pair of Bertone-designed Lamborghinis, the rounded traditional shape of the Giorgetto Giugiaro–Marcello Gandini Miura from 1968 and its successor, Gandini's groundbreaking, angular 1973 Countach LP400.

"I love crisp, taut shapes, but I also love very soft shapes, and hence I always have the Countach and Miura on my favorites list . . . both cars from the same company around a similar time and yet very different expressions."

Hmmm, so look again at the 350Z, a delightfully original design, but note the roundness of the body sides and the fender flares, and then there's the crispness of the headlamps and the detailing . . .

Panchal admits, "Countach was the poster I had all my life--every model I had was a Countach. I remember when I was young, I thought it was the only good-looking car . . . the original." Obviously he has widened his horizons, mixing his love of cars "with the art side. I like sensual shapes, and tactility and texture are very important. But I also like graphic designs."

Ajay Panchal, who was born and educated in England, is given credit for the design of the 350Z. The scale clay model next to him was refined, then used for the car's final shape.

Although he's quite familiar with the use of computers for designing cars, Panchal prefers to begin work on cars like the 350Z in the traditional way, even working on his own small-scale clay models. "I'm very hands-on," he says with a grin. "When I was going through school, the imagery I had in my head was Italy, Italian craftsmen, and the Renaissance artists who had workshops, with people working by hand."

Yet the advance of computer design seems inevitable, and Panchal adds, "The trick is going to be to maintain that handcrafted feeling and sculptural beauty while working on the computer."

So we have an Italian influence on an English-born designer of Indian heritage working for a Japanese company in the United States. Maybe they should change Nissan Design America's name back to the original: Nissan Design International.

2000 Final Design Candidates

By early 2000, the field of potential Z cars had been trimmed still more to a variety of scale model cars from the U.S. and Japanese studios. Ajay Panchal's model, which would become the final Z, is on the top left. Nissan

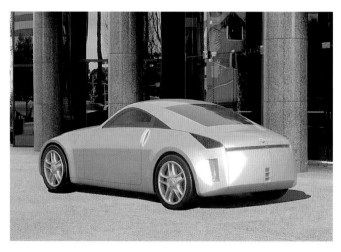

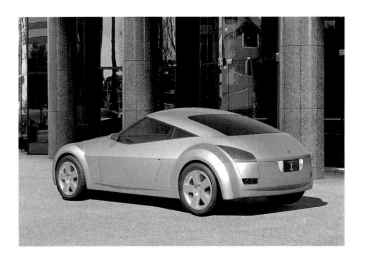

2000 Final Design Candidates (continued)

Shiro Nakamura is the highly regarded designer who heads up design for Nissan and has been responsible for guiding the automaker's new image through the shape of its products. Nissan

2000 Nissan Design American Full-Size Model

Nissan Design America submitted this full-size clay model for the final decision meeting in Japan, March 2000. It is was chosen and, after months of hard work by the company's Japanese studios, transformed into the final production 350Z. Note that the front has two grilles at each side, an idea that was changed into the single center-grille opening. **Nissan**

2000 Nissan Design Japan Full-Size Model

For the March 2000 design decision, Nissan's studio in Japan created this full-scale model, which has a very different approach to the greenhouse glass section. Nissan

What Do You Say, Ajay?

So what goes through the mind of designer Ajay Panchal when he sees a new 350Z drive by?

"It's exciting . . . sometimes I follow it. My joy is also from what a great project it was and what a wonderful team I had to work with. To see what I did to go from paper to reality was wonderful, but so is the reaction of people to the car, which has been very favorable."

It's not unusual for a designer to want to keep fiddling with a design, and, six months after the model went on sale Panchal admits, "I haven't stopped sketching the car now, but generally I'm extremely happy. When you see it outside and moving, it captures all the elements we wanted to do from the beginning. There are details I'd change, but production and cost issues always have to come into account when you do a car, though I think Nissan has been very clever about where to spend the money."

"When we look at a car we often think of it as different 'reads.' There's a first read, a second read, a third read. . . . The first read is big proportion, big picture, how the car is seen on the road, the centerline of the car through the body. Second read would be the surfaces, how beautiful it is, how it flows. The third read is the details and as you walk up closer to it how the details integrate with the other elements. In all those aspects, I feel this car works,

and that, to me, is very satisfying as a designer . . . and for the whole team that worked on it."

He observes, "It's also not a gender-specific car. Some sports cars attract males and others attract females, but this car has a play between machismo and design, but also feminine beauty in a balance on the whole car. There's nothing about it that would make you hate it."

Studio head Diane Allen adds, "The Z draws from no age-specific group. Some owners are guys who owned one when they were young, but also guys who are fanatics because they're tuners." She smiles and adds, "And then there's this group we never expected—kids who are thirteen to fifteen years old, riding their bicycles as fast as they can to catch up to a 350Z because they know it from *Grand Turismo III*."

What's that, you ask? A movie? A television show? Nope, it's one of the hottest-selling video games. Allen explains, "Nissan was smart enough to release the image of Z to the game people before the car was released, so it got in the game, and all these kids know it. The result is this huge, unexpected following that's very exciting." And, no doubt, a generation of kids filing away the name 350Z and, more importantly, perhaps, the name Nissan in their brains for when they reach the car-buying stage.

Right: *The unique door handle is perhaps the most controversial element of the 350Z design. To some, it's a lovely example of detailing. To others, it's too large and prominent.*

Far right: *An example of the design detail that went into the 350Z is this vent that channels air into the door. Rather than being the expected hole, it has "Z" in its grille.*

During one of the design discussions at Nissan Design America, Shiro Nakamura (left), head of Nissan Design, talks with Tom Semple (next to the rear wheel), while other members of the Z design team look on, including Ajay Panchal (second from right). Nissan

2001 Show Car

Nissan showed the 350Z in near-final production form at the 2001 Detroit Auto Show. The main visible differences are in the front end, with the production car having a smaller grille and different turn signals.

5

A New Interior

As Dramatic Inside as Out

Just as the exterior design for Nissan's 350Z was begun at Nissan Design International and then "productionized" in Japan, the sketches that inspired the interior were also first penned at NDI and then finalized in Japan.

Alfonso Albaisa created those initial drawings, and Soichi Maruyama was responsible for working them into final production form. According to Nissan's design chief, Shiro Nakamura, they wanted the interior to be very modern while retaining a hint of heritage, mainly in one important icon from past Z cars: a cluster of three gauges in the middle of the dashboard.

Because the 350Z was the lead car in Nissan's design resurgence, it was meant to help establish a modern design theme inside and out for all sorts of vehicles that would follow, from the Maxima sedan to the Quest minivan and even the company's new full-size pickup truck, the Titan. "We don't want to make them uniform," Nakamura explains, "but consistent, with a family resemblance."

Most important for the Z, the overall feeling of the interior reflects a sports-car attitude, with many of the cues you would expect from a sports machine, such as complete, easy-to-read instrumentation and "tools" such as the steering wheel and shift lever close at hand, all set in a close-coupled, personal cockpit.

Unlike some sports cars, the 350Z is easy to enter, which is helpful when you consider the number of older drivers who will be treating themselves to a Z. Remember, it's on the same platform as the Infiniti G35 Sport Coupe, which shares a great deal with the Z. Although the Z's height is 2.9 inches less than the sports coupe's, it appears to be even less than that.

As you get in the Z, you notice that the driver's and passenger's seats look different. The seatbacks appear similar and, with the seat cushion, are carefully sculpted to support the occupants laterally during hard cornering. Look closely at the driver's seatback, however, and you'll find that the bolstering on the right side is cut away a bit more, to make it easier to shift gears.

The lower cushions are obviously different—the driver's is longer, to support his or her legs, with depressed areas for those legs on either side of what Nissan calls an "anti-submarine" bolster in the middle front of the cushion. ("Submarining" refers to sliding under the seatbelt.) Those cutouts are meant to leave the driver's legs freer to operate the pedals. Yes, this is mostly for visual effect.

The trick is to design a sports car seat that provides the expected lateral support but isn't so firm that it's uncomfortable on long drives. The Z seats achieve this

goal, although as always with such sculpted seats, occupants with wider backs might find them uncomfortable.

Ahead of the driver is a three-gauge pod attached to the steering column that can be adjusted up or down with the wheel. What a driver cares about, of course, is that the display is easy to read. Nakamura points out, "Actually the Z's speedometer and tachometer are quite simple, and that is intentional. We have a more sculptured shape to the instrument pod, and if we made the graphics too expressive, that would make it complicated."

The Z's steering wheel is a variation on one that shows up in many modern Nissans. It's a sports car driver's wheel, shaped to promote keeping your hands at the correct three and nine o'clock positions for fast driving, with integrated cruise control switches. Ahead of the wheel are stalks for the lights and wiper controls, with nicely sculpted twist knobs reminiscent of the design you find on cameras.

Those knobs are just one example of the detailing around the cockpit, such as the creatively shaped door handles. As with those handles, the center console knobs, the drilled pedals, and the shift lever with its padding meant to aid shift feel, it's obvious a lot of time was spent getting the right touch and feel for surfaces used a great deal. Nakamura points out, "In a sports car, you want to be proud of your shift lever, the steering wheel and the gauges . . . driving is everything in a sports car."

An attractive feature of the 350Z, as seen in this profile, is the sense of a close, personal cockpit for the driver and passenger.

Above: *The 350Z with an automatic transmission has a nicely styled shift lever with a left-hand slot that allows manual up- and downshifts.*

Above right: *One of the more unusual design features of the 350Z is the bar that connects the tops of the two rear-suspension struts and spans the luggage area.*

A Cost Balancing Act

All this is well and good, but it creates something of a cost balancing act when a company is trying to create a car built to a price that looks priceless. Nakamura concedes that working to enhance the Z's image while maintaining the car's low sticker price "was tough . . . a big challenge. But from the beginning, we said affordability is the target".

"The cost goal for the interior was tight, but we discussed what parts we should spend the money on. You can see quite a few silver pieces, and they are real aluminum, not fake . . . if you touch them, you can feel that they are cold. Using aluminum is expensive, but we thought we must use it. Just because a car is affordable doesn't mean that it's cheap, and the owner must be proud of it."

One of the hits the 350Z takes from some critics is over the inexpensive look of the finish of some of the materials used in the interior. It's a matter of opinion, of course, but when Porsche introduced its reasonably priced mid-engine Boxster, BMW its Z3, and Honda the S2000, they got the same criticism. Besides, anyone who recalls the early 240Z will remember that its interior materials were certainly specified to a low cost.

There have also been complaints about the lack of a conventional glovebox in the 350Z, though the several covered and lockable bins behind the seats have a total capacity beyond that of gloveboxes. If you happen to use your glovebox every day, the Z might be a problem. If, as with so many owners, it's a once-a-month action, it's nothing of concern.

Optional on the Performance, Touring, and Track models is a DVD-based satellite navigation system with a 7-inch screen. It's not just the usual overhead map view but the slick bird's-eye view, which adds a new perspective to the map.

Touring models come with a thundering 240-watt Bose sound package with seven speakers. The other 350Zs have 160-watt, 6-speaker audio systems.

In the rear under the hatchback is, of course, the controversial brace that spans the luggage area and connects the rear struts, to improve the Z's structural

rigidity. The need for the bar was established early on and with no apologies, because it reflects the sportiness and practicality that are parts of the Z car's heritage. And since the bar was necessary from the start, why not style it to be attractive, complete with a brushed aluminum covering?

Whether you take the Z car on long road trips, use it for weekend entertainment, or need it as a daily driver, the sports car interior fits. Easy entry and exit, an emphasis on the driver's environment, and a long list of amenities as standard equipment in an attractive package make the inside of a 350Z a nice place to be.

Right away, you'll find the 350Z's interior fits comfortably, with no need to adapt to it because it has been designed for you.

Interior Design Sketches

Those who rendered the shift lever worked to mix aluminum and leather for this gear, which is an important point of communication between a sports car and its driver. Nissan

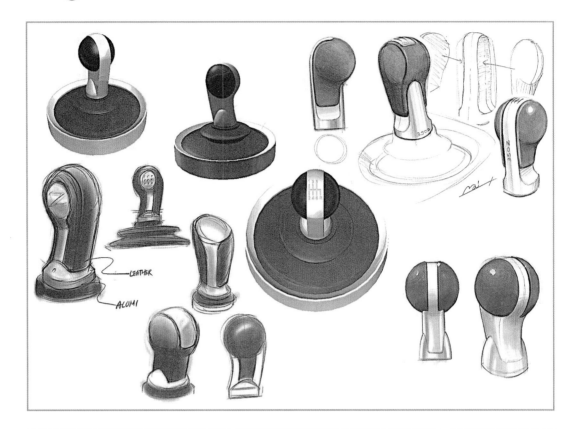

Apparent here is some of the thinking that went into creating the final shape of the 350Z's instrument grouping, which sits neatly just ahead of the steering wheel within easy view of the driver. Nissan

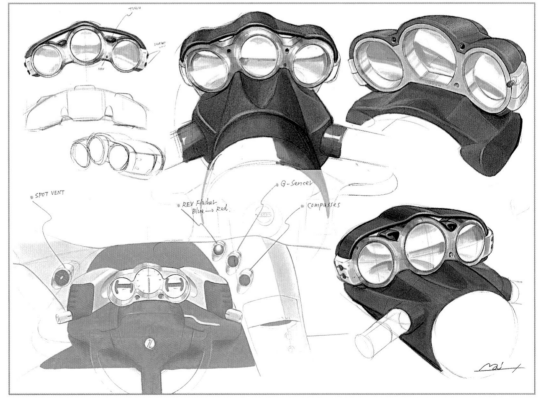

1999 Interior Designs

October 1999 brought dramatic designs, which show the potential style of the Z cars interior. Nissan

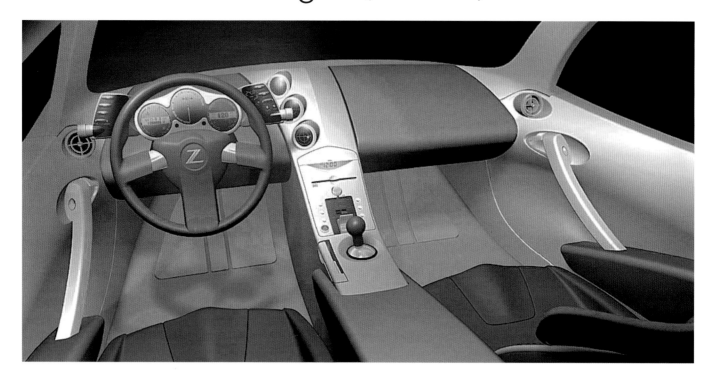

In mid-1999, each of Nissan's design studios gave its interpretation of what a Z interior could look like, with the European treatment finished in tan, the Japanese proposal in solid red, and the American suggestion in maroon. **Nissan**

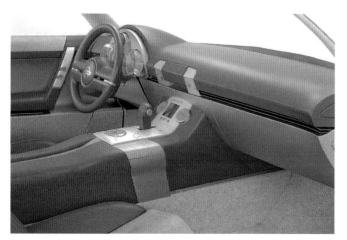

Nissan designers wanted a decidedly driver-oriented cockpit and even gave the pilot a special seat. Notice how the driver's seat has a longer lower-seat cushion, with lower areas on either side of the center pad to allow for more leg movement. At the top of the right side of the driver's vertical cushion, the padding has been minimized to make it easier for the driver to shift.

1999 Interior Designs (continued)

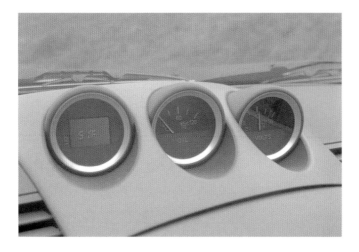

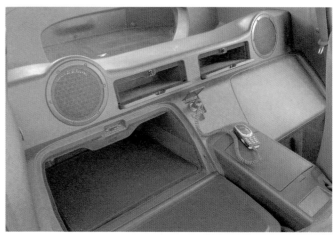

The major design cue carried over from the original Z car to the 350Z is the trio of instruments at the center of the dashboard, which includes readings for oil pressure and voltage.

While the 350Z does not have a conventional glovebox, there are three bins behind the seats—one of them lockable—and a 12-volt outlet for items such as cell phones.

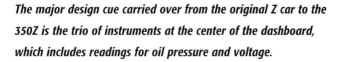

Left: *This is the face of the sound system, which is in the center-console stack. In this case, it is the powerful Bose unit, complete with a six-CD in-dash player.* John Lamm

Left below: *Controls for the heat, ventilation, and air conditioning are three simple knobs that are both attractive and easy to use, even while wearing gloves.*

Below: *Detailing of the 350Z interior includes these metal-faced pedals, which have small rubber sections for excellent grip.*

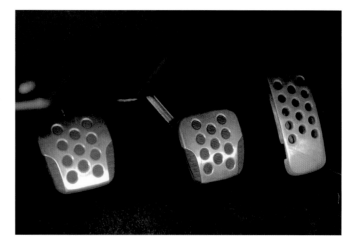

This is the three-pod instrument panel for the 350Z, which contains the speedometer and tachometer plus the fuel and coolant-temperature gauges. To accommodate different-size drivers, it can be adjusted up or down in combination with the steering wheel.

This is the 350Z's instrument display at night. Its red glow makes for easy reading.

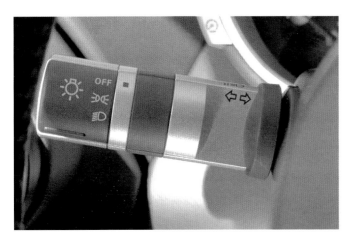

Above: *Details, such as the shift knob, are important to sports car drivers, and this one is well-thought out, even cushioned differently on its sides, front, and back to aid shifting.*

Upper left: *On the left-hand steering-column stalk are the controls for the lights and turn signals. Design of the column levers is said to reflect the look of precision equipment, such as cameras.*

Left: *On the right side of the steering column is a stalk with controls for the windshield wipers and washers.*

1999 Interior Designs (continued)

Despite the bar between the rear-suspension struts, there is a reasonable amount of luggage space under the Z's hatchback, though it's best utilized with soft bags that can be packed around it.

Below: *This steering wheel comes in various forms in many modern Nissans, from the Maxima sedan to Murano SUV. Its design allows the driver to use the classic hands-at-nine-and-three grip.*

Optional on 350Zs is a satellite navigation system. Unlike some other cars' layouts, the Z car's SNS is quite easy to use, thanks to the large, well-labeled buttons, and has a very handy bird's-eye view of the mapped area.

6

Chassis and Development

Under the Skin of the Z

While designers and executives at Nissan in the U.S. were thinking about what a new Z car might look like, engineers in Japan were considering a chassis that could be used under a new generation of Nissans.

Kazutoshi Mizuno, a highly respected chief vehicle engineer at Nissan and team manager of the company's 24 Hours of Le Mans programs from 1989 to 1992, had begun doing some experimental work on a chassis that would be usable for a future sports car. His thinking called for a front mid-engine layout, to provide a car with superior handling. Whether an automobile has a front or rear engine, it is desirable from a handling standpoint to keep the engine as close to the middle of the car as possible.

From a pure handling standpoint, many engineers think the ideal location for the engine is behind the driver: consider Formula 1, CART, IRL race cars, and any number of Ferraris, Lamborghinis, and Porsche Boxsters. Ideal, but impractical for a mass auto manufacturer that would want to use that "platform" for more than one car to spread design and development costs over as many models as possible. Hence Nissan's development of a front mid-engine layout.

In simple terms, think of the platform as just that: a platform fitted with front and rear suspensions, brakes, steering, and other chassis components. This platform can be made wider or narrower, longer or shorter, to form the basis for different types of vehicles.

Mizuno's front mid-engine layout was approved for production under the Nissan code name FM, for a "front midship" layout. This well-executed design would become the mechanical basis not only for the 350Z but also for the Infiniti G35 Sedan and Sport Coupe and the FX45 and FX35 sport utility vehicles, appropriately enlarged and reinforced for the heavier examples. The front midship configuration not only allowed Nissan engineers to create an excellent front/rear weight distribution for the Z of 53 percent front and 47 percent rear, but moving the engine rearward brought aerodynamic benefits.

Welded to this platform is the vehicle's body structure. Crucial to the entire package is the rigidity of that body, because the stiffer the body, the more precisely the suspension is able to work.

Bruce Robinson, an engineer with Nissan's test facility in south central Arizona, was in charge of validating the chassis of the 350Z and the Infiniti G35 Sport Coupe. He

A little fog, a winding road though a pine forest . . . these are the days that offer the chance for an exciting drive.

To give the 350Z and a new generation of Nissan models balance that would lead to well-defined handling, the automaker designed and developed its Front Midship (FM) platform.

and his team not only help create the parameters of what customers want in a new car—Robinson made 15 trips to Japan during the development of the 350Z—but then test what engineers in Japan design and create, to make certain it is appropriate for the U.S. market.

He points out that one of the first challenges with the Z was to get the solid body structure needed to make sure the suspension could do its job—a problem made more difficult by the fact that the Z is a hatchback. The problem could be solved by using thicker-gauge steel for the body, but this brings penalties in weight and detrimental effects on everything from acceleration to handling to fuel mileage.

Nissan's answer to the rigidity question is easily seen by looking in the hatchback window of a 350Z, where you can see a hefty bar with a "Z" in its center that runs between the tops of the rear suspension strut towers. "The bar across the back has been there since the beginning," Robinson explains, adding, "so it was styled in."

A similar bar in the engine compartment ties the front strut towers together, so that the two brace bars can work in conjunction with the platform to create a solid basis for the suspension.

Another important aspect of the Z's solid structure is safety. Design features such as the double-panel floor,

double front bulkhead, and sturdy door sills help create what the company calls a "zone body." This is Nissan-speak for a structure with a strong, central occupant-safety cell that will stand up to heavy crashes, with the front and rear of the car acting as crush zones to absorb impact.

Naturally, the Z comes with driver and passenger dual-stage airbags and safety belts with pre-tensioners, but optionally, you can improve your lot in side impacts with both side airbags and airbag curtains that deploy downward from the base of the headliner, along the sides of the cockpit's "greenhouse."

As with all Z cars, the 350Z's suspension is independent front and rear, today's Z using numerous lightweight aluminum components. The layouts at both ends are what's termed "multi-link" designs with anti-roll bars, the three links in front essentially being a single upper A-arm with the lower "wishbone" split into two arms.

At the back is a four-link-per-side design mounted on an aluminum subframe, which is then bolted to the body. Multi-link means the suspensions are highly tunable, so engineers can give the car a better combination of ride comfort for everyday driving, plus the ability to corner at a high rate for that time when you turn off the normal path and head out on a twisty bit of road. Designed on the computer and tested in thousands of miles of driving, the front suspension is so unique, it earned Nissan 14 patents.

Optional on the Performance, Touring, and Track models is VDC, otherwise known as Vehicle Dynamic Control. This little electronic wonder is able to detect

This is one of the prettiest views of the 350Z, showing the close personal aspect of the cockpit and the Z's nice waistline that ties the front and rear lights together.

Above: *Aerodynamic engineers at Nissan worked with the flow of air over and under the sports car to minimize and balance lift on the 350Z, ensuring its stability at speed.*

Inset: *To make certain the 350Z had a solid body structure despite its hatchback design, engineers decided to add a bar that connects the rear shock towers, which was given a well-designed cover.*

when you are about to go out of control and will dial back the throttle and/or apply any brake as necessary to restabilize the car.

A Tuned and Tunable Suspension

Designing a suspension, with its many links and stabilizer bars, is one thing. Tuning it to what customers will want is another.

John Yukawa, project leader for the Z car, told *Road & Track* magazine's Sam Mitani about the suspension, saying, "My primary goal was to create a car that corners elegantly and effortlessly. I didn't want something that darted into corners like a go-kart, but one that stepped into them in a predictable manner. I wanted the handling feel to be more mature than that of, say, a Honda S2000.

And since we were designing the car primarily for the North American market, we wanted to make sure it was a comfortable tourer."

Bruce Robinson explains, "What was perhaps different on the Z than a lot of recent developments is that this car was tuned subjectively. We did not go in and say we need this percentage increase in stiffness or a skidpad number of 0.9 or anything like that. It was pretty much all by feel. We wanted it to feel and drive and react like a sports car."

As is typical with automakers, they chose "bogies" for the Z, cars in its class that were worthy competitors, with

characteristics consumers seemed to enjoy. "From a chassis standpoint, it ended up being the Porsche Boxster S and the Honda S2000, kind of a blend of those two cars," Robinson explains, adding, "The BMW coupe and Z3 were something we were looking at from an engine standpoint."

Given the differences between the mid-engine Boxster and front-engine S2000, they are an interesting pair for comparison. Robinson explains, "Actually, we shot for a point in between the two of them. The Honda gives the impression of a sports car the minute you drive it away

You can spot a 350Z Track model from a rear view because of the small-lip spoiler that runs across the hatchback lid, which helps cancel rear-end lift at high speed.

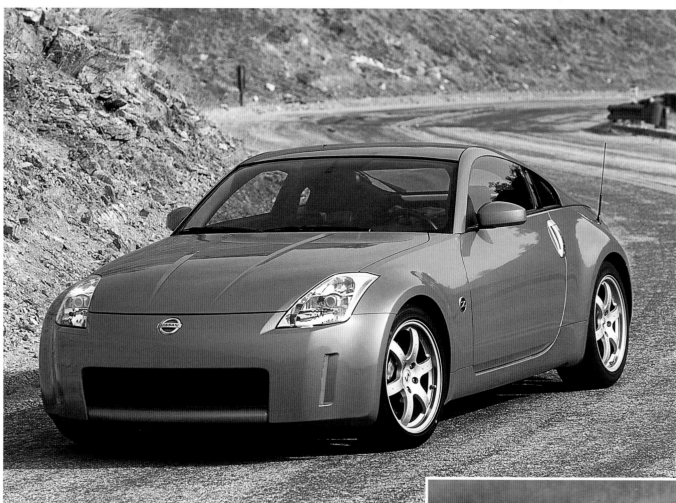

from the dealership. You can't go fifty feet without knowing you're in a sports car. The Porsche is much easier to drive and live with on a day-to-day basis, but maybe isn't quite as exciting around town as you'd like to have it. Once you get out on a highway or curvy road, it's certainly a very capable car."

One interesting result of the Z's development is that engineers homed in on doing just one suspension tuning. It isn't unusual to find you can buy a car with either a base or a "sport" suspension, the latter generally firmer and better handling, but often at the expense of ride quality.

In the Z's case, the suspension is set the same for all six models. The difference comes in tires. Where the Base, Enthusiast, and automatic transmission Touring models have 17-inch wheels and Bridgestone Summer tires (225/50R-17 front, 235/50R-17 rear), the Performance,

manual-gearbox Touring, and Track versions are fitted with Bridgestone Potenza RE 040 Summer tires (225/45R-18 front, 245/45R-18 rear).

One nice little addition on the Performance, Touring, and Track models is a system that keeps track of tire pressure, displaying it on the left-hand upper gauge on top of the dash. Robinson points out that a Z with the 18-inch wheels and tires "does have perhaps a bit more understeer initially, but that allows you to use the throttle more and balance that understeer with the throttle."

The Standard Brakes Are Fine

The one further change with the Track Z is the use of Italian-made Brembo brakes, which seem to glow gold behind the alloy wheels specified for the Track model.

Robinson discusses the brakes, saying, "We did ninety percent of the development on the standard brakes, and we didn't develop them for the track but for the everyday sports car driver. We wanted them to be effective but still at a reasonable cost. I know there have been a couple of complaints in the magazines where after track use the base brakes perhaps started to fade a bit, where the Brembos won't due to their increased capacity, but from a stopping distance standpoint, they're about the same, Brembos and the standard brakes. On mountain road runs the standard brakes are fine, and there is no fade issue."

The Brembo brake option was added for drivers who might like to take their Z to a gymkhana or other driving event where the brakes would take harder-than-usual use.

Under the intake manifold and dress-up panel is the highly regarded V-6 engine that motivates the 350Z, while across it is the strut bar that works with the bar in the rear compartment to give the sports car such a rigid body.

In this cutaway, you can see the basic layout of the Z car's Front Midship chassis, with its multi-link front and rear independent suspensions and engine-speed sensitive power rack-and-pinion steering. **Nissan**

Although the sports car wasn't necessarily designed with racing in mind, the needs of owners who want to use their 350Zs to compete in classes, such as the Sports Car Club of America's Showroom Stock series, were in the back of the engineers' minds. The fact that suspension set points such as camber and caster are fairly adjustable in the car's multi-link suspensions will be a help.

Nissan included 4-channel antilock for the brakes, along with two additions: Electronic Brake Force Distribution (EBD) and Brake Assist. EBD allows for added

loads in the back of the car—say you've stuffed it with heavy bags—and will adjust pressure to the brakes if needed to prevent lockup. Brake Assist can "sense" when the driver has nailed the brakes in an emergency and will add braking power to lower the braking distance.

Developing steering for a sports car can be tricky, because it seems many drivers have different opinions about what is the best balance of effort, feel, directness, and so on.

The steering ratio of the Z's engine-speed-sensitive, power-assisted rack-and-pinion system is 15.9:1. Robinson explains that this "is a little bit slower than the Honda and maybe the Porsche in terms of: if you jerk it thirty degrees on the straightaway, you're not going to get the same rate those two cars have. The Honda in particular gets a little squirrelly at ninety if you start moving the steering wheel around a bit. The quick-response steering they have makes it a lot of fun at forty to fifty miles per hour, but it makes it less stable and certainly less easy to drive on the freeway.

"We wanted something that was fun at forty and at ninety, as this is an everyday sports car, like every Z has been, and we wanted something you could drive on the freeway for hundreds of miles and not be fighting."

An Award-Winning Engine

For an engine, Nissan already had an award-winning solution. Called the VQ35DE, it began as a 3.0-liter engine, enlarged for 2002 to a 3.5. In both forms, the powerplant has been the recipient of a special honor. Since 1994, when the award was first given, the respected *Ward's Auto World* magazine has named Nissan's V-6 to its "10 Best Engines in the World" list.

Left: *This is a close look at the beautifully sculptured reflective surfaces inside the 350Z's headlights, which on all but the base model have Xenon HID low beams and halogen high beams.*

Nissan engineers tuned the 350Z chassis to stay well-balanced and controllable, even on well-used, bumpy tarmac.

Many well-known powerplants have made this tally, from BMW's inline-sixes to the Corvette LS1 V-8, to the Boxster flat-6, to the powerful 2.0-liter engine in the Honda S2000 sports car. But only one engine has been on the list since the honor's inception: Nissan's VQ V-6.

Ward's has called the engine "a marvel of intelligent design and meticulous attention to detail." That design and detail include an aluminum block and cylinder heads, lightweight pistons and connecting rods, and hollow camshafts. With those cams comes the Variable Valve Timing Control System, an invaluable aid in helping engineers give the engine remarkably broad torque and power curves.

Comparing the Z's VQ V-6 to the engine in Honda's popular S2000 Roadster is a good example of two different philosophies in building a modern sports car. Honda's engineers pulled off the impressive feat of developing their sports car's 2.0-liter, 16-valve VTEC 4-cylinder to create 240 horsepower, which is a remarkable 120 horsepower per liter developed up at 8300 rpm. The result is a sports car that's great fun on a race track or an open curvy road.

The problem is that 8300 rpm and that the engine has 153 ft-lb of torque at 7500 rpm, so you need to keep the engine well up the rev band to enjoy the Honda. It's not that much fun around town, and you spend a lot of time shifting through its 6-speed manual transmission, which thankfully has what might be the best production shift linkage in the business.

Nissan's Bruce Robinson points out, "One of the things we gave the Z was a broad torque band, because when you're out just having fun on the road and you're not quite sure what gear you should be in, it's much better to have a broad toque band, so you can motor away, than to have a picky one like the Honda."

So the Z's 3.5-liter V-6 produces 82 horsepower per liter instead of the Honda's 120, but that power is at 6200 rpm and is complemented by a healthy 274 ft-lb of torque at 4800 rpm. Better yet, the engine's torque curve shows it already creates 200 ft-lb by just 1200 rpm and climbs strongly from there. This approach to power means that the VQ engine is easier to use around town and on backcountry twisty roads, where you can spend your time driving rather than shifting.

Despite the 350Z's sub-6.0-second 0 to 60 mph timing, its fuel mileage with the manual transmission, according to the U.S. Environmental Protection Agency, comes in at 20 mpg city, 26 mpg highway, and 22 mpg combined, the automatic transmission losing 1 mpg in the city.

Another little trick in the Z engine: Nissan engineers are aware of the enjoyable aspect of engine sound on sports car drivers and studied the aural effects of such highly prized sports cars as Ferrari's 360 Modena. They then tuned the V-6's intake to provide good, healthy sounds at full throttle in the 3500 to 6000 rpm band and developed the exhaust to thrum its throaty best at 1000 to 3500 rpm, but they set both to be calm and quiet in cruising ranges, when drivers don't want intrusive sounds.

For the Track model, Nissan included Italian-made Brembo brakes. While the stopping distances with the brakes are no better than those of standard discs, their size allows them to be more fade resistant, which is helpful for a 350Z owner who might like to try competitions such as gymkhanas.

Performance, Touring, and Track versions of the 350Z have a tire-pressure warning system that reads out the pressure in the left-most of the three gauges on the dashboard. Here it is displaying the pressures of the rear tires.

Order a Track model and you get Bridgestone RE 040 Summer tires fitted to special alloy wheels, which are only available on this version of the 350Z.

Being a modern sports car, the 350Z does not use a classic cable-operated throttle, but controls the throttle opening electronically "by wire." This has created a new discipline among engineers, who can now adjust the feeling under your foot as you accelerate.

Robinson describes an argument between those who wanted control, feeling, and response that was "impressive around town and those who wanted something that was very controllable at the track and places like that. In the case of the manual, we went with the control side and tried to keep everything linear, so that when you're at half throttle you know it, and you essentially have half the torque left, and when you were at five-eighths throttle you had three-eighths left . . . that type of thing. With the automatic, where it's not quite as racy, we're a little bit early opening, and that gives you more of a boost around town."

Working Your Way through the Gears

Behind the 3.5-liter V-6 is either of two transmissions: a new 6-speed manual or a 5-speed automatic, both developed to suit the 350Z's personality. For example, a critical bit of tuning in any sports car is how the shifting feels. Working your way through the gears is half the fun when driving quickly. Arguably the best-shifting manual transmission in the business these days is the Honda S2000, which Robinson says is, "very good with that snick, snick, snick . . . pretty sporty and one of the things that gives the car a great sports-car image."

He then points out, "You can get short throws and light efforts with low-torque engines (the Honda has 153 ft-lb), but when you go to the torque we have with our V-6 (274 ft-lb), it's just tough to get that light effort. We certainly appreciated the Honda's feel, but it also has some of a small-car feel to it, and we wanted something else." In the end, Nissan engineers "wanted to be better than the Porsche and a little better than BMW and toward the Honda, while realizing we probably couldn't get to the Honda with the torque we're providing."

After development that even had engineers padding the shift lever knob's front and rear surfaces but not its sides just to tailor shift feel, they ended up with what *Motor Trend* magazine's Ron Sessions called, "a short throw wonder that embraces each new gear like an old friend."

Time was when an automatic transmission in a sports car was just an afterthought. Not anymore, not in these days of "intelligent," electronically controlled automatics that give the driver the ability to do crisp manual up- and downshifts. With electronic flexibility comes the ability to more closely tailor the shift characteristics of the automatic transmission. When designing the 350Z's automatic, Nissan baselined against the Boxster and BMW's M3 series but then went a bit further. Robinson says, "We tried to do a couple of other things in the manual shift mode, where we'd keep the torque converter locked up at higher rpm, so you get a more direct throttle-to-throttle feeling, like a manual transmission."

Taking the power from the transmission to the rear differential is a carbon-fiber-reinforced plastic driveshaft. Using this advanced material not only lowers driveshaft weight by 40 percent but also quells noise, vibration, and harshness, because it conducts less of them than a steel driveshaft. In the event of an accident, the plastic driveshaft can break in a controlled manner, to allow the drivetrain to move back and down under the passenger compartment.

On the Base models, the power goes back to a normal differential. Standard for all other Zs is a viscous, limited-slip differential that aids in laying the power down.

Although all these technical components are basically hidden from view, one other aspect is half seen, half unseen. The unseen part is under the car, where all the above components—such as the exhaust system—are packaged to create a flat underbody, to aid smooth airflow under the Z. This airflow is actually "tuned" with such elements as the cover under the engine and the shape of the front bumper, to provide what Nissan calls a "flat ride" that reduces rear-end aerodynamic lift. Add the rear spoiler and diffuser on the Track model and rear lift falls to zero. The car's coefficient of drag, which is 0.30 for the other models, drops to 0.29.

You might have noticed that, as with the rear spoiler that cuts lift to zero, the 350Z's spec list includes any number of performance-enhancing additions, from 18-inch wheels to Brembo brakes to VDC. What makes the Z car unique among many sports cars, however, is that you can be perfectly happy with the basic version. It still has the 287-horsepower engine, the close-ratio 6-speed manual gearbox, the multi-link suspensions, and the 4-wheel disc brakes with ABS.

All the fun comes at no extra charge.

With the Base, Enthusiast, and automatic transmission Touring Z cars, you get these seven-spoke alloy wheels fitted with Bridgestone Summer tires—225/50R-17s on the fronts and 235/50R-17s at the rear.

7

On The Road

Road Tests: Let's Begin with Some Endings

Car and Driver's editor, Csaba Csere, finished the respected automotive magazine's road test of the 350Z with this sentence: "Overall, it's a terrific combination of performance, practicality, style and value. In other words, if you liked the original 240Z, you'll love the new 350."

Motor Trend's Ron Sessions wrapped up their road test by writing: "This is an everyday sports car. It's easy on the wallet from the get-go, reasonably thrifty with fuel, a fast study on challenging sections of road, and practical enough to swallow a fair amount of life's possessions. It's quick when you want it to be, yet smooth as silk on occasions that require discretion. Time will judge whether the Z's controversial sheetmetal wears well. One thing is for sure: The 350Z goes its own way proudly and confidently. Nissan figures there's a significant pool of buyers out there who see things in much the same way."

Those two paragraphs nicely wrap up many of the feelings about the new Z car from those who make their living driving and evaluating new cars.

Some of the more interesting comments are about the 350Z's styling, which ranks as one of the few controversial points on the car.

Personally, I love it. A sports car design needs to be exciting and sit confidently on the road, two things the Z does in spades and from every angle, when approaching, slipping by in traffic, or roaring away from you. Wheels and aggressive tires fill the fender wells—another sports car must—and the overall proportions leave no doubt that this is a personal 2-seater meant just for you and one other.

The interior was designed by people who didn't just study the insides of proper sports cars but who understood what they had studied . . . something that doesn't always happen in car design.

I had my first long exposure to a 350Z while accompanying a colleague from the famous Japanese automobile magazine *Car Graphic*. We spent hours on the freeway, from Southern California well up the state's famous coast. Then we tackled favorite remote roads on what we call the Ferndale Loop, a sinuous bit of coastal pavement that climbs and turns and falls away and has a less than ideal surface that makes for a perfect test road.

Right from the start, you find that the Z car fits you quickly and comfortably, like a favorite pair of shoes . . . probably athletic shoes. No need to break it in, learn what's where, fumble with switches, or adapt to it . . . it's already adapted to you.

Yes, that strut brace gets in the way when loading up, but you just pack for it with soft bags and then find it's

It seems that the 350Z loves being driven, its seats and suspension combining to give a firm but supportive ride whether you are on a winding road or a long, straight stretch of highway.

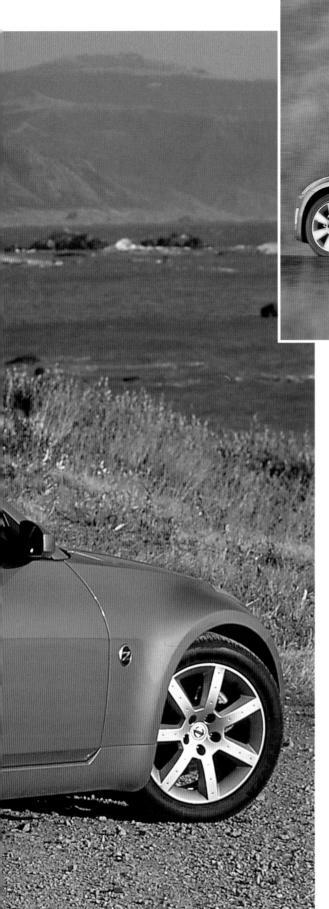

rather handy, keeping larger bags from rolling around in back. We had no trouble hauling along enough clothes and plenty of camera equipment for a four-day trip. Besides, as Nissan's Bruce Robinson pointed out, if you have a technical approach to what's been done to make the Z a better car, the presence of the brace not only isn't a problem, it's easily tolerated in an offbeat sort of way.

Driving many miles on a freeway can be boring in any car, made worse in a rough-riding sports car with overly firm seats. Thankfully, the Z's seats seem to be a comfortable blend of firm and supportive, so you don't end up fidgeting and squirming, wishing to stop and take a stroll.

Nissan seems to have given the Z something of a dual nature, because when cruising, it's a reasonably calm place to be, given its purpose. This is spoiled only on some surfaces when road noise telegraphs into the cabin, and you find yourself reaching for the radio volume knob.

When we finally got a chance to drive it on our favorite test road, the Z's true sports car nature came though. It loves to be driven, and takes to it easily. Turn-in is smooth and precise, and with the linear fly-by-wire throttle, it's easy to apply just the right amount of power. Even on rough, oft-patched stretches, the Z car never loses its composure and stability, staying plastered to the road. You feel you're in harmony, working with the car.

Above: *One of the things that makes the Z so visually impressive is the smart manner in which its wheels fill the wheelwells, giving the car a look of confidence on the road.*

Left: *There's a dual nature to the 350Z, which is ready to be a tiger when it needs to be and willing to play pussycat when appropriate.*

Road & Track's Kim Wolfkill driving the 350Z during its track test. The magazine said of the Z's road manners, "Dynamically, it's tough to fault the Nissan's unflappable handling." Road & Track/Jeff Allen

And, if you just keep your head about you, safe. Some sports cars feel like a weapon in your hands, almost threatening you to drive quickly. Not the Z car, particularly with VDC—it only asks that you not get stupid.

Rushing along on rough roads, you can really appreciate the solid nature of the car. *Car and Driver*— based in Ann Arbor, Michigan, deep in the Midwest, with its bumpy roads—wrote: "The Z's structure is rock solid, never yielding so much as a creak or groan, even when the road surface is an endless series of cracks and pits. The firm suspension always takes the hard edge off the bumps, so you never endure any audible or physical pounding. For a firmly sprung high-performance car, the ride is impressively compliant."

Although it seems like too insipid a way to describe such an exciting car, the word "satisfying" seems to come up a lot. Easy on the eye. A comfortable place to be. A thoughtful cockpit. Ready to be a tiger when you want it or a pussycat when it's appropriate. The Z car is a natural . . . very satisfying.

But how does it compare to the competition? Remember, Nissan targeted the Porsche Boxster as an overall bogie for the 350Z.

Car and Driver: "How does this sound: 0 to 60 mph in 5.4 seconds and through the quarter-mile in 14.1 seconds at 101 mph? How about 0.88 g of cornering stick, a stopping distance from 70 mph to standstill in 164 feet, and a top speed of 156 mph? That's essentially the same performance as a Porsche Boxster S, which has a base price of more than 50 grand.

"Not only is the Z swift in a straight line and around corners, but it is effortlessly so."

Road & Track put the 350Z through a tough comparison, pitting a $34,688 Track model against the Chevrolet Corvette Z06, BMW M3 SMG II, and Porsche 911 Targa. They reported the results in a story titled "David and the Goliaths."

The magazine track-tested the quartet at Willow Springs Raceway, near Los Angeles, then included what it called a "Z Factor"—comparing the new Nissan to much

pricier competition. The Z car got to 60 mph in 5.8 seconds, stopped from 60 mph in 122 feet, generated 0.88 g on the skidpad, and snaked through the 700-foot slalom at 67.3 mph.

Here's what they wrote, and as you read it, keep the Z car's price in mind:

Comparing the 350Z to the BMW M3 SMG II

($55,695, 0 to 60 in 4.9 seconds, 60–0 stopping in 122 feet, 0.89 g on the skidpad, and 68.6 mph through the slalom):

"The Z's V-6 lacks some of the M3's inline-6 smoothness and horsepower, yet enjoys more torque at

Road & Track *pitted the $34,688 350Z against a $55,695 BMW ME SMG II, a $51,450 Chevrolet Corvette, and a $84,975 Porsche 911 at California's historic Willow Springs Raceway. Road & Track/Jeff Allen*

slightly lower revs. The result is an engine that's nearly as powerful at the racetrack, but feels less satisfying and refined around town, where it matters more.

"Inside, the $20,000 price difference becomes more apparent in the quality of the materials. The BMW's cabin doesn't work $20K better, but it's a more pleasant, sophisticated place to spend your daily commute. Poor outward views and little usable space also hurt the Z especially compared with the M3's four seats and trunk.

"Dynamically, it's tough to fault the Nissan's unflappable handling. It's more confidence-inspiring than the M3 (which is saying a lot) with less at-limit understeer and none of the M3's off-throttle oversteer. A little oversteer would actually be welcome at the track, but the setup increases the safety margin for the average driver around town.

"The braking edge goes to the Nissan whose Brembo stoppers posted the exact same braking numbers as the M3, but were more fade-resistant during high-speed use."
Bottom Line: "Similar to the Z in performance, the M3 delivers a more sophisticated driving experience, but at a price premium."

Comparing the 350Z to the Chevrolet Corvette

($51,450, 0 to 60 in 4.5 seconds, 60 to 0 stopping in 114 feet, 0.98 g on the skidpad, and 67.6 mph through the slalom):

"There's little the Z or any other car in this test can do against the Z06's monstrous V-8. Its unrelenting power and bottomless torque make it hard to beat.

"The Corvette requires a careful period of acclimatization before its full performance potential can be realized. The 350Z is almost immediately easy to drive

Road & Track's testers for the Z-car comparison were (left to right) Sam Mittani, Kim Wolfkill, Andy Bornhop, and Doug Kott, here comparing notes in the Willow Springs pits. Road & Track/Marc Urbano

quickly and doesn't demand nearly the same seat time to get comfortably up to speed.

"Both cars share interiors that can't compete with other high-end sports cars. This certainly doesn't affect the performance of either car, but plays a role in the quality of the overall driving experience. At their price points something had to give and better the interior than the mechanicals.

"Under hard acceleration, both cars create quite an interior racket, but in different ways. The 350Z's overly mechanical engine sounds drown out the much more pleasing exhaust note, while the Z06's engine and exhaust work in concert to produce a loud but intoxicating roar.

Bottom Line: "Brothers in arms from a performance versus price standpoint, each delivers impressive performance for the money without the frills of more expensive competitors."

Comparing the 350Z to the Porsche 911 Targa

($84,975, 0 to 60 in 5.0 seconds, 60 to 0 stopping in 120 feet, 0.92 g on the skidpad. and 65.5 mph though the slalom):

"As with the Corvette, driving the 911 takes patience and a period of adjustment. Once mastered, there are few cars as satisfying to drive quickly. The Z suffers from no such waiting period, as it's instantly easy to drive near its limits.

"Its interior may not be nearly as plush as a Porsche's, but for enthusiastic driving, the 350Z's well-bolstered seats, rifle-bolt shifter and idiot-proof handling take the thinking out of logging some fast miles.

"Logging longer, faster miles are right up the 911's alley, where a pleasing driving environment is of greatest importance. Over time, the Z's choppy highway ride and droning engine are no match for the Porsche's proven long-haul credentials.

"If you can afford a 911, odds are good you're not shopping for a Z. But if you are, it's amusing to know you can own a car with nearly the performance of a high-dollar Porsche for about half the cost.

Bottom Line: "Very different cars for very different buyers, but given their respective audiences, each delivers the goods."

Using a financial expression like "bottom line" is appropriate for a discussion of the 350Z. It was a favorable bottom line on the price sticker of the 240Z that made it such a hit and the first page in the Z legend. The price so amazed us just over 30 years ago that we easily overlooked the car's shortcomings, charmed by its newness, its great fun. It was an unfavorable bottom line that killed the 300ZX, as Nissan descended into a seemingly bottomless black hole.

It seemed almost in defiance of a bottom line that the new Z project was begun. And yet here we have it, as charming a bargain as the first Z car—the real bottom line being that it is, quite simply, one helluva car.

G35 versus 350Z

While Nissan developed both 2-place and 2+2 versions of past Z cars, don't wait up for a new 350Z 2+2. In several of Nissan's markets, however, there's something just as good. In the U.S., it's called the G35 Sport Coupe and is sold by the automaker's Infiniti luxury division.

When developing its FM (front midship) platform, Nissan did both the 104.3-inch wheelbase Z version and the longer 112.2-inch G35 coupe edition. Overall lengths are different—169.6 inches for the sports car, 182.2 for the coupe—and the Z is 2.9 inches lower, but both are 71.5 inches wide, and they share the same front and rear track. Where Z cars weigh in between 3,188 and 3,247

From the side, you can see more of a Nissan family resemblance in the 350Z and G35 Sport Coupe,
particularly in the shape of the greenhouse and the car's overall proportions.

A head-on view highlights the G35's unique personality. The design of this and all Infinitis is meant to be more classic, as they are more expensive machines, while the Nissans are more cutting-edge.

pounds, the coupe is 3,416 to 3,435 pounds, each with a 53/47 weight distribution.

Both cars use Nissan's award-winning 3.5-liter aluminum 24-valve V-6. Horsepower and torque are slightly different, the Z's 287 horsepower versus the coupe's 280, while at 274 ft-lb, the sports car has 4 more foot-pounds of torque. Both offer 5-speed automatic and 6-speed manual transmissions, with identical gearbox and final drive ratios.

Styling-wise, the Japanese-designed G35 is a sophisticated tourer, the California-done Z a big-wheel athlete, its design meant to make a strong statement about the rebirth of once ailing Nissan. Their characters are different enough that if you weren't aware of their common background, you wouldn't necessarily place them from the same company.

Inside, the G35 has generous 2+2 seating, much more than in the cursory rear seats of the earlier Z-car 2+2s. Those G35 rear seats also look like they were designed as part of an entire interior rather than having the added-on look seen in the old Z cars.

Nissan did an excellent job with the interior design of the G35 Sport Coupe, which is more traditional and highly detailed; the only real tie to the Z car is the steering wheel.

It's the same engine as in the Z car, but hiding under its own nicely styled cover. While the Z's 3.5-liter V-6 has 286 horsepower and 274 ft-lbs of torque, the G35 claims 280 horsepower and 270 ft-lbs.

Unlike many 2+2 coupes that offer only tiny rear seats, the G35 Sport Coupe's are quite generous in size. There's also a surprising amount of headroom.

If you know Nissans, you can see the interior tie between the Z and G35, starting with the multifunction steering wheel used in many of the company's products, including the Murano SUV. No complaints, by the way, as it's a very effective wheel, with radio controls on its face. Also obvious—and handy—is that the steering column and three-gauge instrument pod are up-down adjustable, moving as one piece.

The driving difference? Both cars are strong off the line, the G35 coupe's time to 60 mph around 6 seconds, the Z a few tenths of a second quicker. Both can be driven hard along winding roads, their differences more from the coupe's extra length, weight, and the visual character of the interior rather than what you feel through your backside. The coupe is arguably a somewhat better-riding car than the sports car, thanks in part to its longer wheelbase.

Another important difference is in road noise. The Z is more of a growler, a feisty street fighter ever ready to show its prowess, with a firm, sometimes noisy ride and a demeanor that's always a bit on edge. The coupe also has an edge, but it's more of a use-it-when-you-want-it thing. There's also a calmer tone (the feminine side?) to the coupe that's welcome on long rides.

Although U.S. Z prices start at $26,269, the ones most buyers want are in the $28,000 to $29,000 range, which is where G35 Sport Coupe costs begin. While the sports car builds to the raucous Brembo-braked Track model at $34,079, the G35 aspires to leather trim and more civility at $32,050, though we see at least another $3,500 in options we'd like.

Two exciting automobiles that are surprisingly different, considering their common roots.

If you'd like one of this pair but must have four doors, Nissan has another answer: the G35 sedan. Visually, there's no mistaking the tie between the G35 coupe and the sedan—they're like two very attractive, visually similar, differently configured peas from the same pod. Both ride on an identical 112.2-inch wheelbase, the sedan measuring 4 inches longer but weighing about 100 pounds less.

Again the driveline carries over from the Z car and G35 Sport Coupe, though the sedan's horsepower and torque are a bit lower still, with 260 horsepower and 260

ft-lb. Underneath is the same all-independent multi-link suspension and 4-wheel disc brakes with ABS. Now the engine noise and suspension tuning are more in keeping with the family car image—but although the G35 sedan is less athletic than the coupe and sports car, it still has a slight edge to it . . . something that nicely sets this 4-door apart from the competition.

It's also the sort of difference that, combined with its attractive exterior design, has new car buyers walking happily through the door who previously wouldn't even have known where the Infiniti dealer was located. The G35s has impressed journalists too, with the Infiniti G35 sedan and Sport Coupe jointly winning *Motor Trend*'s 2002 Car of the Year award. The G35 sedan and 350Z were two of the three finalists for the highly regarded North American Car of the Year.

That's not all. If you feel the need to own an SUV—or want one to supplement your 350Z—the Infiniti FX35 has the same VQ V-6 engine and is based on the FM platform, with just a change in the front suspension to allow for the option of 4-wheel drive. It's basically a 350Z SUV . . . what a concept.

Not bad for Nissan, a company that just four years previously was bleeding money.

GReddy, a well-known aftermarket engine firm, added a pair of Mitsubishi turbochargers and an intercooler to a Z's V-6, along with a new intake manifold, which bumped horsepower to 345 through the stock catalytic converters.

As soon as the Z was launched, there was a line of extras offered by Nissan Motorsports (NISMO), many of which were used on several cars shown at the 2002 SEMA show in Las Vegas.

Among the Nissan Motorsports' (NISMO) extras are LM GT-4 alloy wheels, a low back-pressure exhaust system that increases horsepower, and S-tune suspension modifications that include new shocks, springs, and anti-roll bars.

Aftermarket Options

For many who buy a 350Z, the finished car will be just about perfect. They might get a Z key chain, pop for a Fossil Z-car watch, or purchase a nose bra or car cover to protect the paintwork, but to them the car is just fine the way it is.

For others, their new 350Z is like an empty canvas: where to begin?

With the new 350Z, it all began at something called the SEMA show. The letters stand for Specialty Equipment Market Association, and at one time that meant hot rodders. These days, it's a showcase for the wares of a multibillion-dollar industry devoted to spiffing up cars, whether you're just looking for new wheels or want to set a new record in a quarter-mile drag race.

Held each November in Las Vegas, the show fills that city's convention center. In 2002, just months after the 350Z's first sales, the Z was *the* hottest new car in the show. Zs were featured in exhibits throughout the halls,

James Chen, of Axis, added a set of his own Axis S7 modular wheels, which not only look good but also make it easier to see the big Brembo brake calipers fitted to this Track model.

Below: *Axis fitted the Z with an aero kit from Wet Works and then had the car painted PPG yellow, with a bit of gold pearl added. Suspension changes include HKS coil-over springs and shocks.*

Above: *In addition to painting many of the inside surfaces the same yellow as the exterior, Axis swapped the stock passenger seat for the same type as the driver's.*

Right: *Axis used the rear spoiler sold by Nissan Motorsports (NISMO) for its yellow Z. Nissan concluded that many owners might not fix up their car immediately, but perhaps after they've owned it for a while.*

Painted bright yellow and riding low on its suspension, big alloy wheels a blur, the Axis Z car has the sort of look many owners will opt for as they spiff up their own Zs.

with some of the most important on Nissan's own stand. There sat three tricked-out Zs, two done by the company, finished off with NISMO parts. This is important, because NISMO (NISsan MOtorsports) has just begun to import its own parts and pieces for the company's products.

Most obvious at the 2002 show was a NISMO aero kit with a new front fascia, side skirts, and a rear spoiler. Yokohama tires were fitted to NISMO LM GT-4 alloy wheels. A NISMO Weldina stainless–catalyst, low-back-pressure exhaust system ups horsepower from the stock 287 to 295, torque from 274 ft-lb to 280, and sounds growly. Also fitted to the engine were such upgrades as a low-restriction air filter element, an air-to-oil engine cooler, a cooler for the power steering oil, a lightweight flywheel, a special clutch disk, and a limited-slip

differential. The suspensions featured NISMO's S-tune equipment, which includes shocks, springs, and anti-sway bars to firm up the handling.

Nissan recognizes, however, that some owners will want to go to other suppliers for pieces for their Z cars, because individualization is at the heart of dressing up your personal car. So they sent a car off to Axis Sport Tuning in nearby Whittier, California. There, James Chen added the NISMO rear spoiler and a Wet Works aero kit, then painted the Z PPG chrome yellow, mixed with a bit of gold pearl. The wheels are his own Axis S7s, open enough to allow the yellow-painted Brembo brake discs to show through. The suspension features HKS coil-over springs and shocks.

The engine is another typical place for aftermarketeers. While 0 to 60 mph in under 6.0 seconds

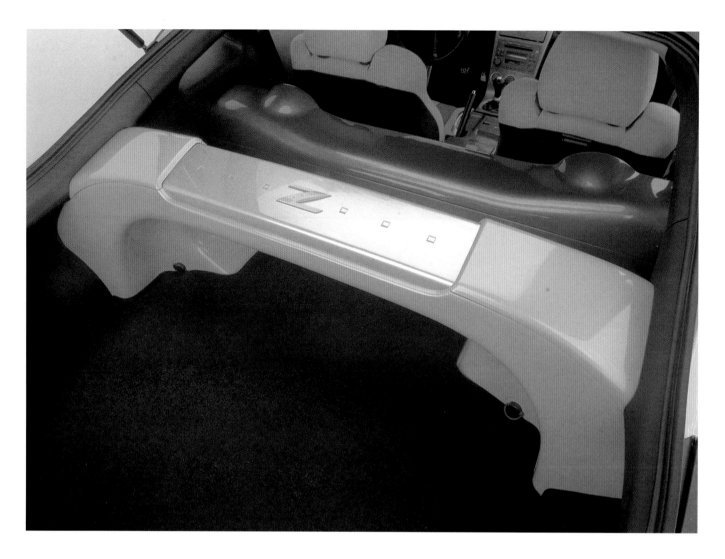

should be (and probably is) enough power to satisfy most Z car owners, that doesn't stop them from asking for more. It is also why a turbocharged Z car from Nissan is a good bet for a future upgrade. Not only does it fit in nicely with a heritage of turbo Zs, it keeps the line new and fresh.

But some owners just don't want to wait, and by the SEMA just months after the car's debut, turbo kits were already being proposed. Well-known engine tuner GReddy showed a 350Z with a turbo kit with a pair of Mitsubishi turbos, an intercooler, new manifolds, and all the bits and pieces needed to boost the Z's horsepower from the stock 287 to some 345 through the stock catalytic converters.

For the interior, owners can get custom upholstery kits for under $1,000, as well as additional sound equipment and thick floor and trunk mats.

As each month goes by after the launch of the new Nissan, more and more accessories become available. But if production of aftermarket pieces lags behind the introduction of the 350Z, that's okay, because sales of these accessories might, too. While some new Z owners will want to immediately add spoilers, new wheels, and such, as Nissan Z car product planner Joel Weeks points out, "A year from now, as the car ages, as the new owner gets a promotion, he can afford that $2,000 wheel and tire kit, and the next year the body kit. We've learned from our research that as they move forward with the life of their car and they earn more money, owners will buy more things as well."

And to go with the 350Z is an extensive line of non-car items that broadcast ownership. For as little as under $15 there's a hat, then comes the $30 sweatshirt, the $50 jacket—or, better yet, the $200 jacket. Wallets, pens, and

Inevitably, the 350Z will be raced, though the initial problem is finding the appropriate series for the new sports cars. This is Nissan Motorsports' (NISMO) idea of what a race version looks like. **Nissan**

duffel bags—the latter handy when packing around the rear strut bar—can be had for less than $50. Nissan will also make a specific set of luggage available, able to fit maximum loads around the bar.

The list goes on, from wallets to CD cases to thermal coffee mugs, all emblazoned with the Z logo. And since you can't drive the car all the time, the famous Japanese model company, Tamiya, makes a terrific scale model that would look just right on your desk.

Remember, cars like the 350Z, Porsche Boxster, Honda S2000, and BMW Z4 are more than just automobiles . . . they're a lifestyle.

Index